FAITH AND POLITICS

BENEDICT XVI
JOSEPH RATZINGER

Faith and Politics

Selected Writings

With a Foreword by Pope Francis

Translated by Michael J. Miller and others

IGNATIUS PRESS   SAN FRANCISCO

Cover design by Roxanne Mei Lum

© 2018 by Ignatius Press, San Francisco
ISBN 978-1-62164-230-5
Library of Congress Catalogue number 2018939113
Printed in the United States of America ⊗

CONTENTS

FOREWORD

by

His Holiness Pope Francis

The relation between faith and politics is one of the major themes that have always been at the center of attention of Joseph Ratzinger—Benedict XVI throughout his entire intellectual and human career: his firsthand experience of Nazi totalitarianism led him even as a young student to reflect on the limits of obedience to the state for the sake of the liberty of obeying God: "The state", he writes along these lines in one of the texts presented in this volume, "is not the whole of human existence and does not encompass all human hope. Man and what he hopes for extend beyond the framework of the state and beyond the sphere of political action. This is true not only for a state like Babylon, but for every state. The state is not the totality; this unburdens the politician and at the same time opens up for him the path of reasonable politics. The Roman state was wrong and anti-Christian precisely because it wanted to be the totality of human possibilities and hopes. A state that makes such claims cannot fulfill its promises; it thereby falsifies and diminishes man. Through the totalitarian lie, it becomes demonic and tyrannical."

Later on, again precisely on this basis, at the side of Saint John Paul II, he elaborates and proposes a Christian vision

Translated by Michael J. Miller.

of human rights that is capable of calling into question
at the theoretical and practical level the totalitarian claim
of the Marxist state and of the atheistic ideology on which it
was founded; because in Ratzinger's opinion the real contrast between Marxism and Christianity certainly does not
consist in the Christian's preferential option for the poor:
"We must also learn—again, not just theoretically, but in
the way we think and act—that in addition to the Real
Presence of Jesus in the Church and in the Blessed Sacrament, there is that other, second real presence of Jesus in
the least of our brethren, in the downtrodden of this world,
in the humblest; he wants us to find him in all of them",
Ratzinger writes as early as the 1970s with the theological
depth and at the same time the immediate accessibility that
are characteristic of a genuine pastor. Nor does that contrast consist, as he emphasizes in the mid-1980s, in a lack
of a sense of equity and solidarity in the Church's Magisterium; and, consequently, in denouncing "the scandal of the
shocking inequality between the rich and poor—whether
between rich and poor countries, or between social classes
in a single nation—[which] is no longer tolerated."[1]

The profound contrast, Ratzinger notes, consists
instead—even prior to the Marxist claim to place heaven
on earth, man's redemption in the present world—of the
fathomless difference that exists between them with regard
to *how* redemption is supposed to come about: "Does
redemption occur through liberation from all dependence,
or is its sole path the complete dependence of love, which
then would also be true freedom?"

And thus, thirty years in advance, he accompanies us
in understanding our present day, which testifies to the

---

[1] Congregation for the Doctrine of the Faith, Instruction on Certain Aspects
of the "Theology of Liberation", August 6, 1984, no. 1.6.

unchanged freshness and vitality of his thought. Today, indeed, *more than ever*, the same temptation is being proposed again: to reject any dependence of love that is not man's love for his own *ego*, for "the I and its desires"; and, consequently, the danger of the "colonization" of the conscience by an ideology that denies the fundamental certainty that man exists as male and female, to whom is assigned the task of transmitting life; the ideology that goes so far as to plan rationally the production of human beings and that—perhaps for some end that is considered "good"—goes so far as to think it logical and licit to eliminate what it no longer considers to be created, given as a gift, conceived, and generated, but considers, rather, to be made by ourselves.

These apparent human "rights", which all tend toward man's self-destruction—Joseph Ratzinger shows us this forcefully and effectively—have one common denominator, which consists in one great denial: the denial of the dependence on love, the denial that man is God's creature, lovingly made by him in his image, for whom man thirsts like the deer for running streams (Ps 42). When this dependence of the creature on the Creator is denied, this relation of love, one basically relinquishes man's true greatness and the bulwark of his liberty and dignity.

Thus the defense of man and of what is human against the ideological reductions of power proceeds today once again by way of establishing man's obedience to God as the limit of obedience to the state. To take up this challenge, in the truly epochal change through which we are living today, means to defend the family. Elsewhere, Saint John Paul II had already understood correctly the decisive importance of the question: it was no accident that he, who was rightly called also the "pope of the family", stressed that "the future of humanity passes by way of the family."[2] And along this line I, too, have stressed that "the welfare of the family is decisive for the future of the world and that of the Church."[3]

Thus I am particularly happy to be able to introduce this second volume of selected writings of Joseph Ratzinger on the theme of "faith and politics". Together with his weighty *Complete Works*, they can help all of us not only to understand our present day and to find a sound orientation for the future but also to be a true and genuine source of inspiration for political action that places the family, solidarity, and equity at the center of its attention and of its planning and thereby truly looks to the future with far-sighted wisdom.

Franciscus

---

[2] Pope Saint John Paul II, Apostolic Exhortation *Familiaris Consortio* On the Role of the Christian Family in the Modern World, November 22, 1981, no. 86.

[3] Pope Francis, Post-Synodal Apostolic Exhortation *Amoris Laetitia* On Love in the Family, March 19, 2016, no. 31.

PREFACE

The Multiplication of Rights and the Destruction of the Concept of Law

Points for a discussion of Marcello Pera's book *La Chiesa, i diritti humani e il distacco da Dio* *(The Church, Human Rights and Estrangement from God)*

No doubt your book is a major challenge for contemporary thought, and particularly for Church and theology, too. The hiatus between the statements by the popes of the nineteenth century and the new view beginning with *Pacem in Terris* is well known and widely discussed. Indeed, it is one of the core issues in the opposition of Lefebvre and his followers to the council. I do not feel capable of giving a clear answer to the set of problems raised by your

This text by the Pope Emeritus, sent by him to Prof. Marcello Pera on September 29, 2014, is published here by the kind permission of both. The book by Marcello Pera, published in 2015, bears the definitive title *Diritti umani e cristianesimo: La Chiesa alla prova della modernità* (*Human rights and Christianity: The Church put to the test by modernity*) (Venice: Marsilio, 2015). The title given here to the essay by Benedict—"The Multiplication of Rights and the Destruction of the Concept of Law"—is editorial and was taken from the text. The original text had as its title what is printed here as the subtitle. Translated by Michael J. Miller.

book but, rather, can only note a few aspects that in my estimation could be important for further debate.

1. Only through your book did it become clear to me what a new trend begins with *Pacem in Terris*. I was aware of how strong the effect was on Italian politics, in which this encyclical gave the decisive impetus for the *Democrazia Cristiana* party to open up to the left. I was not aware, however, of the extent to which it also signaled a fresh start in the fundamentals of its thought. Nevertheless, to my recollection, the question of human rights first took on an important role, practically speaking, in the Magisterium and in postconciliar theology through Pope John Paul II. My impression is that with the saintly pope it was less the result of reflection (which of course was not lacking in his case) than it was the consequence of practical experience. He regarded the idea of human rights as the specific weapon against the totalitarian claim of the Marxist state and of its founding ideology, an idea that limits the totality of the state and thus offers the necessary free space not only for personal thought but above all, too, for the faith of Christians and the rights of the Church. The secular paradigm of human rights, as it had been formulated in 1948, plainly appeared to him to be the rational counterforce against the all-encompassing ideological and practical claim of the state founded on Marxism. Thus, as pope, he mobilized worldwide against all sorts of dictatorships the concern for human rights as a power acknowledged by universal reason. This operation was directed no longer only against atheistic dictatorships but also against states with religious foundations, as we encounter them above all in the Islamic world. The fusion of politics and religion in Islam, which necessarily restricts the freedom of other religions, and thus of Christians, too, is contrasted

with the freedom of religion, which now to a certain extent also views the secular state as the correct form of government that allows room for the freedom of religion that Christians have claimed from the beginning. In precisely this regard, John Paul II knew that he was also intrinsically in continuity with the early Church. She was faced with a state that, although it was quite familiar with religious tolerance, still clung to an ultimate identification of governmental and divine authority, which Christians could not endorse. The Christian faith, which proclaims a universal religion for all mankind, thus necessarily included a fundamental limitation of the state's authority through the right and duty of the individual conscience. At this point, though, the idea of human rights had not been formulated. It was instead a matter of contrasting man's obedience to God with obedience to the state as a limit on the latter. But it seems to me that it is not unwarranted to formulate man's duty to obey God as a right vis-à-vis the state, and in this respect, it was probably quite logical when John Paul II found in the Christian relativization of the state for the sake of freedom to obey God the expression of a human right that preexists all state authority. In this sense, the pope, in my estimation, was by all means able to maintain that the fundamental idea of human rights is in intrinsic continuity with the Christian tradition, even though the linguistic and conceptual means are quite disparate.

2. In my estimation, the doctrine that man is made in the image of God contains in this matter what Kant expressed when he described man as an end and not a means. One could also say that it contains the fact that man is a subject of rights and not only an object of law. In Genesis 9:5–6, this elementary core of the idea of human rights, so it seems to me, is expressed clearly: "For your lifeblood I

will surely require a reckoning; ... of every man's brother I will require the life of man. Whoever sheds the blood of man, by man shall his blood be shed; for God made man in his own image." The fact that man is made in the image and likeness of God includes the fact that his life is under God's special protection—that, prior to any human legislation, he is the holder of a right enacted by God himself.

This view acquired foundational importance at the beginning of the modern era with the discovery of America. Since all the newly discovered peoples were not baptized, the question arose whether they had any rights at all. According to the prevailing opinion, they became actual subjects of rights only through baptism. The recognition that due to creation they were God's image and remained so even after original sin suggested at the same time the insight that they were already subjects of rights even before baptism and could make a claim to respect for their humanity. It seems to me that "human rights" were recognized here that preexist the acceptance of the Christian faith and all governmental authority of whatever sort.

If I see it correctly, John Paul II understood his commitment to human rights as being in continuity with the attitude of the early Church toward the Roman state. In fact, the Lord's commission to make all nations his disciples created a new situation in the relation between religion and state. Until then there was no religion with a claim to universality. Religion was an essential part of the identity of the particular society in question. Jesus' commission does not directly signify the demand for a change in the structure of individual societies. But it demands that in all societies the possibility of acknowledging his message and living by it remain open. With that, first of all, the essence of religion is newly defined: it is not a rite and observance that ultimately guarantee the identity of the state. Rather, it is knowledge (faith) and, indeed, knowledge of truth. Since the human mind is created for truth, it is clear that the truth obliges (though not in the sense of a positivist ethics of duty but, rather, by its very nature) and that in precisely this way it makes man free. This association of religion and truth includes a right to freedom that may be seen in an intrinsic continuity with the true core of the doctrine of human rights, as John Paul II obviously saw it.

3. You correctly presented the Augustinian idea of state and history as being fundamental and made it the basis of your view of the Christian doctrine on the state. Perhaps, though, the Aristotelian vision, too, would have deserved even more attention. As far as I can see, in the Middle Ages, of course, it was scarcely brought to bear in the Church's tradition, especially after its acceptance by Marsillius of Padua came into contradiction with the Church's Magisterium. Then, since the nineteenth century, it has been taken up all the more in the development of Catholic social teaching. A twofold *ordo* is now assumed: the *ordo naturalis* and the *ordo supernaturalis*, whereby the *ordo naturalis* is regarded as being complete in itself. It is explicitly emphasized that the *ordo supernaturalis* is freely added and signifies sheer grace, which cannot be demanded in terms of the *ordo naturalis*. With the construction of the *ordo naturalis*, which is to be understood in a purely rational way, an attempt was made to acquire a basis for argumentation on which the Church could introduce her ethical positions into the political debate in a purely rational way. What is correct about this view is that even after original sin the order of creation, although wounded, is not completely destroyed. To assert what is truly human, when the claim of faith cannot and should not be made, is in itself an appropriate position. It corresponds to the autonomy

of the realm of creation and to the essential freedom of faith. In this respect, a deeper vision of the *ordo naturalis* reflecting creation theology is justified, indeed, probably necessary in connection with the Aristotelian doctrine of the state. Of course there are dangers, too:

a. It is very easy to forget the reality of original sin and to arrive at optimistic positions that are naïve and do not do justice to reality.

b. If the *ordo naturalis* is regarded as a whole that is complete in itself and not in need of the Gospel, there is a danger that what is distinctively Christian might appear to be an ultimately superfluous superstructure over natural humanity. In fact, I can remember that once the draft of a document was submitted to me in which pious phrases did appear at the end, but during the whole course of the argument not only Jesus Christ and his Gospel but even God was missing and thus appeared superfluous. Apparently, the authors thought that they could construct a purely rational order of nature, which then, however, is not rationally compelling after all and, on the other hand, threatens to relegate what is distinctively Christian to the realm of mere sentimentality. In this respect, the limit of the attempt to elaborate a self-contained, adequate *ordo naturalis* becomes clearly visible here. Father de Lubac, in his book *Surnaturel* [*The Mystery of the Supernatural*], tried to prove that Thomas Aquinas himself, who is cited in this regard, did not mean it quite like that.

c. One substantial problem with such an attempt is that when one forgets the doctrine of original sin, a naïve confidence in reason results that does not perceive the actual complexity of rational knowledge in the ethical realm. The drama of the dispute about the natural law clearly shows that the metaphysical rationality that is presupposed here is not evident without further ado. It seems to me that in his later works, Kelsen was right when he said that it is reasonable to derive an Ought from what Is only if someone deposited an Ought in the Is. Of course, for him this hypothesis is not worth discussing. In this respect, it seems to me, nevertheless, that everything ultimately depends on one's concept of God. If God exists, if there is a Creator, then one can also speak about *his* Is and demonstrate to man an Ought. If not, then ethics is ultimately reduced to what is pragmatic. This is why, in my preaching and in my writings, I have always insisted on the centrality of the question of God. It seems to me that this is the point in which the vision of your book and my thought are fundamentally in agreement. The idea of human rights holds up in the final analysis only if it is anchored in faith in the Creator God. From there it receives its limit and at the same time its justification.

4. It occurs to me that in your book *Perché dobbiamo dirci cristiani* [*Why We Should Call Ourselves Christians*], you evaluate the idea of God of the major liberal thinkers differently from the way you evaluate it in your new work. In your new *opus*, it already appears essentially as a step toward the loss of faith in God. In your first book, in contrast, you had shown in a way that for me was convincing that European liberalism is incomprehensible and illogical without the idea of God. For the fathers of liberalism, God was still the foundation of their view of the world and of man, so that, according to this book, the logic of liberalism makes necessary precisely this acknowledgment of the God of Christian faith. I understand that there are good arguments for both evaluations. On the one hand, in liberalism, the concept of God is detached from its biblical foundations and thus slowly loses its concrete force. On the other hand, for the major liberal thinkers, God

still remains indispensable nevertheless. We can emphasize one or the other side of the process more. I think that we should mention both. But the vision of your first book remains indispensable for me, namely, that liberalism loses its own foundation when it leaves God out.

5. The concept of God includes a basic concept of man as the subject of rights and, thus, at the same time, justifies and limits the idea of human rights. In your book, you have presented strikingly and convincingly what happens when the concept of human rights is detached from the concept of God. The multiplication of rights leads finally to the destruction of the concept of law and ends in a nihilistic "right" of man to deny himself—abortion, suicide, and the production of a human being as a thing become rights of man that at the same time deny him. Thus, in your book, it becomes convincingly clear that when separated from the concept of God, the concept of human rights finally leads not only to the marginalization of Christianity but ultimately to its denial. This—in my estimation, the real concern of your book—is, in view of the present intellectual development in the West, which increasingly denies its Christian foundation and turns against it, of great significance.

Vatican City, September 29, 2014
Benedict XVI

I

The Good Friday of History

I

In the great *Passions* by Johann Sebastian Bach that stir us anew each year during Holy Week, the awful event of Good Friday is bathed in transfigured and transfiguring beauty. Admittedly, these *Passions* do not speak of the Resurrection—they end with the burial of Jesus—but their purity and nobility are derived from the certainty of Easter, the certainty of a hope that is not extinguished even in the night of death.

Nowadays, however, this confident and tranquil faith that does not need to speak of the Resurrection, because it lives and thinks in its light, has become strangely alien to us. In the *Passion* of the Polish composer Krzysztof Penderecki, the tranquility of a community of believers who live constantly in the light of Easter has disappeared. Instead, we hear the tortured cry of the persecuted at Auschwitz; the cynicism and brutal commando voices of the masters of that hell; the eager voices of the hangers-on as they join in the screeching, thus hoping to rescue

"Gekreuzigt, gestorben, auferstanden", in vol. 6.2 of the *Gesammelte Schriften*, ed. Gerhard Ludwig Müller (Freiburg et al.: Herder, 2008–). Translated by Michael J. Miller as "Good Friday", in Benedict XVI/Joseph Ratzinger, *Dogma and Preaching* (San Francisco, 2011), 287–94.

themselves from the terror, the lashing whips of the anon-ymous, omnipresent power of darkness, the hopeless sighs of the dying.

This is the Good Friday of the twentieth century: the face of man is mocked, covered with spittle, beaten by man himself. From the gas chambers of Auschwitz; from the ruined villages and outraged children of Vietnam; from the slums of India, Africa, and Latin America; from the concentration camps of the Communist world that Solzhenitsyn has brought before our eyes with such pas-sionate intensity: from every side the "bleeding head sore wounded, reviled, and put to scorn" gazes at us with a realism that makes a mockery of any aesthetic transfigura-tion. If Kant and Hegel had been right, the progress of the Enlightenment should have made man ever freer, more reasonable, and more upright. Instead, the demons we had so eagerly declared dead rise ever more powerfully from the depths of man and teach him to feel a profound anx-iety at his own power and powerlessness: his power to destroy, his powerlessness to find himself and master his own inhumanity.

The most terrible moment in the story of Jesus' Pas-sion is doubtless the one in which he cries aloud in his extreme torment on the Cross: "My God, my God, why have you forsaken me?" The words are from a psalm in which Israel—suffering, oppressed, scorned because of its faith—cries out its need before the face of God. But this cry of supplication, uttered by a people whose election and communion with God seem to have turned into a curse, acquires its full dreadfulness on the lips of him who is him-self the redemptive nearness of God in the midst of men. If *he* is conscious of being abandoned by God, then where is God still to be found? Does not this moment mark, in all truth, the darkening of the sun of history, the hour in which the light of the world is extinguished? Today, the echo of this cry, magnified a thousandfold, rings in our ears from the hell of the concentration camps, from the battlefields of the guerilla wars, from the slums of the starving and despairing: "Where are you, God, that you could create such a world, that you can look on while your most innocent creatures often suffer the most terribly, as sheep are led to the slaughter and cannot open their mouths?"

Job's ancient question has acquired an edge hardly ever matched in the past. Often, of course, the question is asked rather arrogantly, and behind it can be glimpsed a sense of malicious satisfaction, as when student newspapers repeat in overbearing tones what the students have had preached to them: that in a world forced to learn the names of Auschwitz and Vietnam, no one can seriously talk any longer of a "good" God. But the insincerity that is all too often evident does not make the question any less valid. For in this our own hour of history, we all seem for practical purposes to be contemporaries of Jesus at the point when his Passion turned into a cry to the Father for help: "My God, my God, why have you forsaken me?"

What can we say in response to this cry? In the last analysis, the question Jesus asked is not to be answered with words and arguments, for it penetrates to a depth unfathomable to mere reason and the words that such reason produces. The failure of Job's friends is the inevitable lot of all who believe they can answer the question, positively or negatively, with clever thoughts and words. No, the question can only be endured, suffered through—with him and at the side of him who suffered it to the end for all of us and with all of us. An arrogant sense of having dealt adequately with it—whether in the spirit of the student newspaper or in the spirit of theological apologetics—can only miss the real point.

It is possible, nonetheless, to make a couple of suggestions. The first thing to be noted is that Jesus does not declare the absence of God but, rather, turns it into a prayer. If we want to unite the Good Friday of the twentieth century with the Good Friday of Jesus, we must integrate our century's cry of distress with Jesus' cry to the Father for help and transform it into a prayer to God who is nevertheless near to us. You may, of course, go a step farther and ask: "Is it possible to pray honestly as long as we have done nothing to wipe the blood from those who have been beaten and to dry their tears? Is not Veronica's gesture the least that must be made before there can be any talk of prayer? Can one pray at all with the lips alone, or does not that always require the whole person?"

But let us content ourselves with this first suggestion, which leads us to reflect on a second one: Jesus has truly entered into and shared the affliction of the condemned, while we—most of us, at least—have on the whole been only more or less involved onlookers at the horrors of the twentieth century. This fact is connected with an observation of some importance: remarkably enough, the claim that there can no longer be any God, the claim, that is, that God has completely disappeared, is the urgent conclusion drawn by *onlookers* at the terror, the people who view the horrors from the cushioned armchair of their own prosperity and attempt to pay their tribute to it and ward it off from themselves by saying, "If such things can happen, there is no God!"

But among those who are themselves immersed in the terrible reality, the effect is not infrequently just the opposite: it is precisely then that they discover God. In this world of suffering, adoration has continued to rise up from the fiery furnaces of the crematories and not from the spectators of the horror. It is no accident that the people who in their history have been the most condemned to suffering, the people who have been the worst battered and the most wretched and who did not have to wait for 1940–1945 to be in "Auschwitz", also became the people of revelation, the people who have known God and made him visible to the world. And it is no accident that the man who has been the most afflicted and has suffered most— Jesus of Nazareth—was and is the revealer, nay, revelation itself. It is no accident that faith in God flows from a "head sore wounded", from a crucified man, and that atheism has Epicurus for father and originates in the world of the satisfied onlooker.

The awful and threatening gravity of a saying of Jesus that we usually set aside as inappropriate suddenly comes home to us here: A camel will sooner pass through the eye of a needle than a rich man enter the kingdom of heaven. Rich man? That means anyone who is well-off, saturated with prosperity, and knows suffering only from television. We should not be too ready to dismiss these words of Jesus, which are a warning to us, especially on Good Friday. Admittedly, we need not and, indeed, must not call down suffering and affliction on ourselves. Good Friday is something God imposes when and where he wishes. But we ought to learn even more fully—not only theoretically, but in our practical lives—that every good thing is a gift on loan from him and that we must account for it before him. We must also learn—again, not just theoretically, but in the way we think and act—that in addition to the Real Presence of Jesus in the Church and in the Blessed Sacrament, there is that other, second real presence of Jesus in the least of our brethren, in the downtrodden of this world, in the humblest; he wants us to find him in all of them. To accept this truth ever anew is the decisive challenge that Good Friday presents to us year after year.

2

The image of the crucified Christ that stands at the center of the Good Friday liturgy reveals the full seriousness of human affliction, human forlornness, human sin. And yet down through the centuries of Church history, the crucifix has constantly been seen as an image of consolation and hope.

Matthias Grünewald's *Isenheimer Altar*, perhaps the most deeply moving painting of the crucifixion that Christendom possesses, stood in a monastery of the Antonian Hospitalers, where people were cared for who had fallen victim to the dreadful plagues that afflicted the West in the late Middle Ages. The crucified Jesus is depicted as one of these people, his whole body marred by the plague-boils, the most horrible torment of the age. In him the words of the prophet are fulfilled, that he would bear our griefs and carry our sorrows.

Before this image, the monks prayed along with their sick, who found consolation in the knowledge that in Christ God suffered with them. This picture helped them realize that precisely by their illness they were identified with the crucified Christ, who in his affliction had become one with all the afflicted of history. In their cross, they experienced the presence of the crucified Jesus and knew that in their distress they were being drawn into Christ and, thereby, into the abyss of everlasting mercy. They experienced his Cross as their redemption.[1]

In our day, many have grown deeply mistrustful of this understanding of redemption. Following Karl Marx,

[1] See A. Zacharias, *Kleine Kunstgeschichte abendländischer Stile* (Munich, 1957), 132.

they see the consolation of heaven in recompense for the earthly vale of tears as an empty promise that brings no improvement but only renders permanent the world's wretched state and, in the last analysis, benefits only those in whose interest it is to preserve the status quo. Instead of heavenly consolation, then, these people call for changes that will remove and, in this sense, redeem suffering. Not redemption through suffering, but redemption from suffering is their watchword: not expectation of help from God, but the humanization of man by man is the task for which they call.

Now of course one could immediately retort that this sets up a false dilemma. The Antonians quite obviously did not see in the Cross of Christ an excuse for not engaging in organized humanitarian aid addressed to special needs. By means of 369 hospitals throughout Europe, they built a network of charitable institutions in which the Cross of Christ was regarded as a very practical summons to seek him in those who suffer and to heal his wounded body; in other words, to change the world and put an end to suffering.[2]

We may ask, moreover, whether amid all the impressive talk about humaneness and humanization that we hear around us there is as real an impulse to serve and assist as there was in those days. One frequently has the impression that we want to buy our freedom from a task that has become too burdensome for us by at least talking grandly about it; in any case, we get along today in large measure by borrowing people for service roles from the poorer nations, because in our own country the impulse to serve has grown weak. But still we must ask how long a social organism can survive when one of its key organs

---

[2] See K. Hofmann, article "Antonianer", in *Lexikon für Theologie und Kirche*, 1:677.

is failing and can hardly be replaced over the long term by transplantation.

Admittedly, then, even—and especially—with regard to the activity required if we are to shape and transform the world, we must disregard the facile contrasts that are fashionable today and view the question differently. But by doing that, we have still not fully answered the questions we are discussing here. For, in fact, the Antonians followed the Christian creed in preaching and practicing not only redemption from the Cross but also redemption through the Cross. To do so is to bring out a dimension of human existence that increasingly eludes us today but nonetheless constitutes the very heart of Christianity; in its light alone are we to understand Christian activity for and in this world.

How can we come to see this heart of the matter? I will try to suggest a way by referring to the development of the image of the Cross in the work of a modern artist who, though not a Christian, was increasingly fascinated by the figure of the Crucified and was constantly trying to grasp the essence of it. I am referring to Marc Chagall.[3] He first depicts the crucified Jesus in a very early work that was painted in 1912. Here the entire composition forces us to think of him as a child; he represents the suffering of the innocent, the undeserved suffering in this world that by its very nature is a sign of hope. Then the crucified Jesus disappears completely from Chagall's work for twenty-five years; he reappears only in 1937, but he now conveys a new and more profound meaning.

This triptych on the crucifixion had a remarkable predecessor, another tripartite painting that Chagall later

[3] For the following description, cf. H.-M. Rotermund, *Marc Chagall und die Bibel* (Lahr, 1970), 111–38.

destroyed but of which an oil sketch in colors has survived. That earlier picture was entitled "Revolution". On the left, there is an excited crowd waving red flags and brandishing weapons; by this means, the revolution as such is brought into the picture. The right side contains images of peace and joy: the sun, love, music; the idea is that the revolution will produce a transformed, redeemed, restored world. In the center, linking the two halves, is a man doing a handstand. Clearly, there is a direct allusion to Lenin, the man who symbolizes the entire revolution that turns things upside down and transforms left into right; the kind of total change that leads to a new world is taking place.

The picture recalls a Gnostic text from the early Christian period in which it is said that Adam, that is, mankind, stands on his head and thus causes up and down, left and right, to be reversed; a complete conversion of values—a revolution—is needed if man and the world are to become what they should be. We might call this picture by Chagall a kind of altar to political theology. Just as he had expected the Russian Revolution of 1917 to produce salvation, so after this first disillusionment, he placed his hopes a second time in the French Popular Front that had come into power in 1937.

The fact that Chagall destroyed this picture shows that he buried his hopes a second time and probably for good. He painted a new triptych that has the same structure: on the right, a picture of the salvation that is coming, but purer and less ambivalent than before; on the left, the world in turmoil, but now marked more by suffering than by conflict and with the crucified Jesus hovering over it. The decisive change, and one that gives a new meaning to the two side panels, is to be found at the center: replacing the symbol of the revolution and its delusive hopes is the colossal image of the crucified Jesus. The rabbi, representing the Old Testament and Israel, who had previously sat at Lenin's side as if in confirmation of his work, is now at the foot of the Cross. The crucified Jesus, and not Lenin, is now the hope of Israel and the world.

We need not inquire to what extent Chagall in his own mind was intending to adopt the Christian interpretation of the Old Testament, of history, and of being human in general. Quite independently of the answer to this question, anyone who sees the two pictures side by side can derive an unambiguously Christian statement from them. The salvation of the world does not come, in the final analysis, from a transformation of the world or a political system that sets itself up as absolute and divine.

We must indeed go on working to transform the world, soberly, realistically, patiently, humanely. But mankind has a demand and a question that go beyond anything politics and economics can provide, that can be answered only by the crucified Christ, the man in whom our suffering touches the heart of God and his everlasting love. Indeed, man thirsts for this love; without it, he remains an absurd experiment despite all the improvements that can and should be made.

The consolation that goes forth from him who bears the stripes meant for us is something we still need today, in fact, today more than ever. In all truth, he is the only consolation that never degenerates into an empty promise. God grant that we may have eyes to see and a heart open to this consolation; that we may be able to live within it and pass it on to others; that during the Good Friday of history we may receive the Easter mystery that is at work in Christ's Good Friday and, thus, be redeemed.

II

Salvation: More than a Cliché?

Redemption is a key word of the Christian faith; it is also one of the Christian words that has been most emptied of meaning: even for believers, it is difficult to discover another reality behind it. When they compare the drudgery of their daily lives, its battles, anxieties, and uncertainties, with the Christian Good News, often it seems to them almost impossible to acknowledge this redemption as something real. Furthermore, the words in which the faith tradition speaks here—atonement, vicarious substitution, sacrifice—have become obscure; all that verbiage produces no true connection with the experiences and insights of human existence today. It has been more than fifty years now since Josef Wittig, the Catholic theologian from Breslau, formulated this feeling in a way that, because of its artlessness and frankness, was felt by many to be a true liberation. At that time, he recounted how as schoolchildren they had received an explanation of the doctrine of redemption and had learned to sing the song, "Getröst, getröst, wir sind erlöst" ("Comforted, comforted, we are redeemed")—but this pious poetry, which really says nothing to anyone, was suddenly interrupted by

"Erlösung—mehr als eine Phrase?", in vol. 6.2 of the *Gesammelte Schriften*, ed. Gerhard Ludwig Müller (Freiburg et al.: Herder, 2008–), 943–54. Translated by Michael J. Miller.

the very impudent question of an inquisitive little pupil:
What, then, are we actually redeemed from? Answer:
From sin—but that did not satisfy the little rascal, because
all of religious instruction deals with sin, which means
that really we are not totally redeemed from it. The next
answer given to the little boy, though, threw the system
completely out of gear: Well, we can confess our sins now
and receive forgiveness in the confessional. There was no
answer to his final thoughtful question: Maybe, instead of
redeeming us from sin, shouldn't Christ have redeemed us
from confession?

Basically, such ridicule is still harmless; in Wittig's case,
its primary purpose was merely to suggest a more relaxed
way of practicing Christianity, with more trust and candor.
Of course, behind it something deeper is noted: we have
a sense that, actually, we do not have to be redeemed by
Christianity but, rather, from Christianity; there is an insistent feeling that, in truth, Christianity hinders our freedom
and that the land of freedom can appear only when the
Christian terms and conditions have been torn up. Amid
the hopes that sprang up at and around the Second Vatican
Council, a very similar mixture of motives was at work.
Here, too, initially the expectation of a simpler, more
candid, and less regulated Christianity gave wings to the
hope that in this way one could again unearth the ruined
joy of the Gospel. But immediately it became obvious
that behind a loosening of dogma and behind the abandonment of confession, the promised land of the happy
freedom of the redeemed does not appear—far from it—
but, rather, a waterless waste that only becomes ghastlier
the farther one walks. The landscape now on display was
mapped by Jean-Paul Sartre with the crystal-clear logic
that is characteristic of Gallic wit. In the migration out of
the realm of Christian tradition, Sartre had already taken

the final step: to him it is clear that the real constraint of all man's constraints is God; in casting off inhibiting ties, man has not done the decisive deed until he has rid himself of this fetter. God's nonexistence, he says, is the prerequisite for human freedom, for if there were a God, then indeed the space of human existence would be predetermined by him and obedience would be the inescapable fundamental condition of our lives. Nothing set in advance, but only if there is no God; then there is no idea of man as creation, no nature of man that predetermines for him who or what he is and ought to be. With that, he is then in fact completely free; everyone must invent for himself what he thinks it means to be human, and no standard limits him when he does. "Man is what he makes himself to be"; so the French thinker formulates the quintessence of his philosophy of freedom. But this complete freedom is the opposite of redemption. Man is the unhappy being that does not know what it is, what it is for, what it is supposed to do with itself. In the ocean of nothingness, he must first plan what he wants to be, because the fact that there is no idea of him naturally implies also that there is no meaning. Freedom from God is logically freedom from meaning, too: meaninglessness. The freedom that Sartre discovers is in truth man's condemnation: animals simply are what they are, and they are happy; man, who must make himself, is precisely for that reason in hell—he himself is hell to himself and to the other.

At this point we can recall again either the point of departure with Wittig or else a remark found in Kurt Tucholsky's *Letters to a Catholic Woman*. The woman correspondent, who was appalled by his mockery of what to her was great and holy, had tried to bring him to the point where the Christian message would necessarily affect him, too. She had referred to what in her opinion was

the primordial human and inescapable theme of redemption and said: "But, after all, that concerns everyone." But
it was impossible to upset the assurance of Tucholsky's
ironic thinking; quite unimpressed, he answered: "You
really have to get used to the fact that there are very con-
tented pagans; that does not concern them at all.... In
me there is nothing that has to be redeemed; I do not feel
this *culpa* [guilt], maybe some other kind.... Nothing at
all concerns me. Nothing."[1] Let us leave aside here the
fact that for Tucholsky himself paganism very soon lost its
cheerfulness; after all, that may have been due to a merely
external incident. In Sartre's case, in contrast, the interior
migration of paganism, the exodus from the constraints of
faith and Church into complete "freedom", was accomplished down to the last possible boundary, and behold:
freedom from God proves to be man's hell, which, in fact,
strangely enough, agrees exactly with the old definition of
hell. But might Sartre just have lacked the right program
in order to give meaning to this freedom? Certainly, it
is no coincidence that, in his bare abandonment in the
wilderness of nothingness, he ran across the man who a
hundred years earlier had already thought such thoughts
and elaborated them into a program for human liberation.
In the writings of Karl Marx we read the propositions: "A
being is only considered independent once it stands on its
own feet, and it only stands on its own feet once it owes
its existence to itself.... A man who lives at the mercy
of another regards himself as a dependent being. My life
necessarily has a reason outside of itself unless it is my own
creation."[2] The argument that Marx uses here to develop

---

[1] Kurt Tucholsky, *Briefe an eine Katholikin 1929–1931* (Reinbek: Rowohlt,
1970), 62.

[2] Karl Marx, *Ökonomisch-philosophische Manuskripte aus dem Jahre 1844*, in Karl
Marx and Friedrich Engels, *Werke*, Ergänzungsband I (Berlin, German Democratic Republic: Dietz Verlag, 1968), 465–588 at 544f.

his groundbreaking view of liberation and man's salvation is altogether sensible: If I have to expect redemption from someone else, I am dependent. If I am dependent, I am not free. If I am not free, I am also exposed to uncertainty. After all, I cannot do the decisive deed myself; whether the other does it is not up to me—it just might not occur. If I am not free and uncertain, then I am unredeemed. Therefore the decisive thing must be to overcome all dependence. Liberation from all dependence—in essence, liberation from waiting for God—must then be the heart of any theory of redemption, which itself, consequently, shows the way for the praxis of redemption and turns into it:

If that is how it is, then redemption can be brought about only by smashing dependencies, by doing and not by waiting or receiving.

Christian faith and logically consistent paganism along the lines of Marx and Sartre thus have in common the fact that they revolve around the theme of redemption, but in exactly opposite directions. It immediately becomes evident that the real difference does not lie in the question of whether redemption is thought of as being earthly or heavenly, spiritual or secular, otherworldly or this-worldly. These alternatives, which usually dominate the field, are far too shortsighted and conceal the real problem. They are only imprecise consequences of the real alternative: Does redemption occur through liberation from all dependence, or is its sole path the complete dependence of love, which then would also be true freedom? Only from this perspective is the true difference made clear in practical decisions. If redemption means that being under orders or indebted in any way must be overcome as a demeaning lack of freedom, then the praxis of emancipating deeds necessarily follows from this immediately; then I must try to bring about conditions in which no one needs to thank anyone anymore but, rather, in which each one now stands on his own. Someone who refuses, however, to let the indebtedness of love be slandered as dependency that is contrary to freedom, someone who sees precisely therein the liberating fulfillment of man—he must walk a different path. He must, first of all, increase man's interior depth and open him up to true love; he must struggle for the mind and heart of man. This by no means makes his activity merely spiritual and merely otherworldly: it will be much more present to man today, much more directly related to his here and now than the other program, which does have its heaven on earth but in a future that is much farther away from the present than the heaven of faith, which always stands over the earth and takes aim into its today. We must go another step farther. "A being ... only stands on its own feet once it owes its existence to itself",[3] Karl Marx had said. This is logical, no doubt. But is it also true? Can my life ever be my own creation, so that it does not have to thank any other creator? Can the emancipation of man from God, from his Creator, ever lead anywhere but into untruth? And can untruth be freedom? Here we must appeal to the modest authority of common sense: it cannot go well if man tries to claim for himself a freedom that fundamentally contradicts his own truth and if he constructs the program of all his activity on this denial of the truth.

If that is the case, then man's salvation must look different. In one respect, it will be less simple. It cannot take place in such a way that the good world is produced like a technological working part through planned partisan effort. It will take away from no one the adventure of being human. It will not be programmable at all in

---

[3] Karl Marx, *Ökonomisch-philosophische Manuskripte*, 544f.

advance from outside, because it concerns man personally, in his guilt and in his love. But for precisely this
reason, it will not be the endlessly postponed day after
tomorrow, either, which can be built only upon the rub-
ble of what went before and is heralded for the time being
only through a zeal for destruction. It will have to be
more modest and at the same time greater. It will have
to mean first, then, that man no longer needs to be afraid
of God. As long as the power that reigns throughout the
world, that confronts us in the forces of the universe and
of the earth, remains unknown and wordless, it is strange,
dangerous, sinister for us—also and precisely when it is
denied. This power is for man the quintessence of dominion, distance, and, thus, of his own helpless subjugation.
Technology is an attempt to banish this dominion of the
unknown, to domesticate the power of the universe and
to leave no unknown power, no untamed force behind.
No longer should the universe rule over man but, rather,
only man over himself. But this is precisely the cause of
the situation that agitates us most today: man's dominion over man. When the universe no longer rules, man
is abandoned to the rule of man, which can often be
much more sinister and allows us to see the abysses of
uncontrolled power only from the other side. The first
thing that would have to happen, if redemption were to
exist, would therefore be this: that God no longer be the
Unknown, the Immovable, the Untouchable; that he no
longer be the limit of our freedom, the competitor with
our own life. He himself would have to be one with us,
if we were supposed to be free. Again—the aim of technology and politics is to make man his own god; but there
is a desperate illogic in such attempts, as we saw. No. In
order for that to work, it would have to come from God
himself; he would have to make himself one with us; he

would have to stop being the unknown, the overwhelming Lord. Only then would it really work.

A second thing that we must demand in order for redemption to exist would be this: man's yearning for love would have to lose its uncertainty, the quiet impossibility of ever fulfilling it. Even amid the wreckage of human associations, man would have to be able to know inviolably that he is accepted, that someone says Yes to him. He does not need the undetermined freedom of nothingness—the assurance that no one willed him, no one made him—but, rather, the determined freedom of knowing that he is willed, that he, he specifically, is needed and unconditionally necessary. He yearns for the certainty that love does not lead to emptiness, that we all do not exist separately alongside each other with no possibility of being united, but, rather, that there is a union going down to the foundations that cannot be destroyed and really corresponds to my yearning for fulfillment. Only when man knows that this is how it is with him, that everything fickle, unpredictable, and uncertain in his being-loved disappears, only then is he free. The opposite way, to cast off love so as not to be abandoned to its uncertainty, is an operation, so to speak, that is performed at the expense of the patient's life: it amputates precisely what makes man human.

When we pace out the dimensions of our life and of its questions, we run into another further realm that cannot be pushed to one side. Solzhenitsyn gave literary expression to it with his characteristic passion in his novel *Cancer Ward*. He writes:

> "What do we keep telling a man all his life? 'You're a member of the collective!' ... That's right. But only while he's alive. When the time comes for him to die, we release him from the collective. He may be a member, but he has

to die alone. It's only he who is saddled with the tumour, not the whole collective. Now you, yes, you!"—he poked his finger rudely at Rusanov—"come on, tell us, what are you most afraid of in the world now? Of dying! What are you most afraid of talking about? Of death! And what do we call that? Hypocrisy!"[4]

What matters to Solzhenitsyn here? The collective, the community of providing, having, and making, sustains man in his work; it sustains him in his life, insofar as it is identical with his work. But this sustaining community abandons him precisely where he would need it most; when his work stops and when he himself is what matters. In reality, the loneliness of death and suffering only uncovers what is already true throughout life. When death finds no meaning, then life, too, becomes brittle. When suffering finds no answer, man is left abandoned precisely where his questioning begins in earnest. Someone who can reply to a person's suffering only with the prospect that one day it will be over and done with has nothing to say in this decisive matter. On the contrary, with such information, he declares suffering to be utterly meaningless and thus gives it its destructive cruelty. What a person needs would be a community that sustains him even in death and can make his suffering meaningful.

Finally, the problem of guilt remains. One of the depressing aspects in the experience of being human is that our power to destroy is far greater than our power to heal. The outstanding debt of guilt extends farther than the radius of forgiveness and reparation. The irrevocable drilling power of guilt still preys on people today; it leaves psychiatrists

---

[4] Aleksandr Solzhenitsyn, *Cancer Ward*, trans. Alexander Dolberg (London: Random House, 1968, 2011), 152–53.

and counselors of all sorts ultimately helpless, because guilt cannot be absolved by knowledge or removed by analysis. It calls for an authority of transformation that goes beyond human ability.

With all that, we have said nothing specifically Christian. These are the questions that have beset the history of religion in every age; the questions that show the real explosive force in societal problems. These are the questions on which is based also that despair of our century from which Marxism draws its strength, which in purely logical terms would be utterly incomprehensible: no man by himself can contradict the fear of God. No man can reform the insecurity of our existence that is grasping for love. No collective can intrude upon death. Absolving guilt is not in our power. This is why to so many people the only possibility seems to be to challenge all this from the bottom up and to tear it down, to cast aside God, love, guilt, and death and, instead, to work to create a new world in which all this can no longer occur. But this promise remains illusory, and it only shreds the remnants of what in spite of everything can make life bearable.

Once again: all these questions are not specifically Christian, and, nevertheless, in them we have actually already developed in question form the entire content of the figure of Jesus Christ. Let us go right to the center, to his death. Those who have experienced this death have recognized more and more deeply that his dying was ultimately the act of love that he himself performed, in which he distributed himself, communicated himself completely to his disciples. And this showed that this act of love was in the most profound sense the deed of the love of God himself, in which he, as man, overcame the limits of human love with the power that belongs to God alone. Death, the illogical, the unspiritual and senseless, thus becomes an active spiritual event. Death, the end of communication, becomes here an act of communion pure and simple: of Jesus with everyone and, in him, of everyone with everyone and of God through Jesus with everyone. At the very place that is the concentrated expression of man's lack of freedom and of his helplessness, which no one can remove, he is liberated; indeed, he actually can be liberated in truth only when the center of alienation itself, the center of his lack of freedom, is transformed and the door is kicked open here: in the realm of the power of death. In it, however, the one who is for him the quintessence of power and of his own helplessness, the mysterious Lord of the world, becomes loving-kindness that distributes itself, that gives itself as a gift. God is no longer the sinister one, the abyss of an ultimate fear that nothing can resolve; he has become "like us", and he waits in death as love, as the Yes that overcomes guilt and banishes uncertainty in that reliable kindness which alone is freedom.

Now one may say: All that sounds very nice, and if it were true, then that really would be the redemption of the world. But is it true? Can we believe it? Why do we see so little of it? I would like to reply with a statement from above, from the perspective of God's logic, and with a statement from below, from the perspective of the logic of being human. Viewed from above, this is true: the God who redeems, the God who liberates, cannot act like the God who creates things out of nothing. That in itself would be illogical. God cannot enter into man's already existing freedom in the form that is ordered to the creation of being but not to the togetherness of persons. This entrance can occur only in the manner in which persons are capable of entering into one another, that is, by way of being for each other and its opening love, which demands faith in advance. Omnipotence here can take effect only in the universal force of vicarious substitution, in the God-man's Being-for-us. That means, from below, from our own perspective, that one cannot buy redemption, so to speak, ready-made off the rack; one must enter into it with the whole path of one's human existence. In the second century, Irenaeus of Lyon explained this, with an urgency that has scarcely ever been equaled, to the Christians of his time, who had grown impatient. On all sides, he had to listen to rebellion against the Christian message of redemption, against its historical patience and against its human demands.

Rebellion against the drudgery of the process of Christian education, which does not grant the redemptive wishes that man has in mind. In his writings, he recorded the question: Could God not make man perfect from the beginning? Is he not himself responsible for human unhappiness? The succinct answer of the Church Father reads:

> Before that they become men, they wish to be even now like God their Creator, and they who are more destitute of reason than dumb animals [insist] that there is no distinction between the uncreated God and man, a creature of to-day. For these [the dumb animals] bring no charge against God for not having made them men.... For we cast blame upon Him, because we have not been made gods from the beginning, but at first merely men, then at length gods.[5]

And another passage reads: "But if you are ungrateful to Him, because you are a mere man, then you have cast

---

[5] Irenaeus, *Against Heresies*, IV, 38, 4, in ANF 1:522a.

aside His creative power and life itself. For creating is an attribute of God, but becoming is that of man."[6]

The yearning to become like God has seethed mightily in man ever since his origin; indeed, the yearning to be one's own creator now and not to be obliged to thank anyone anymore is ultimately nothing but the clamoring demand to have no more God but, rather, to be a god for oneself. About this, Irenaeus says: It is correct that man is supposed to become like God and cannot rest until he has attained the freedom of sonship—that alone can be the freedom appropriate for him; that alone can be his redemption. But he cannot be God; he can only become like him, and he cannot become godlike if he tries to extinguish divinity in a violent grasp for divinity. This is directed against a pedagogy of emancipation that smashes the virtues of a developing, maturing human being; naturally it is directed also against dysfunctional forms of Christian education. When the supernatural is sought, not in promoting human existence, but rather in suppressing it, then it is just as true as at the other extreme: before they are men, they already want to be gods. It is clear for Irenaeus that man *is* not but, rather, *becomes*; hence in the individual, there is a process of education, of advancing step by step, of gradual formation, even through failures. Because its goal is maturity, that is, full freedom, the equality with God that is sonship, therefore such education for God can be achieved only by God, and our equality only through his becoming equal to us. For this reason, Christ, God-made-man, is man's only chance, his true and sole-sufficient redemption. For

---

[6] Irenaeus, *Against Heresies*, IV, 39, 2. Translated from German. Cf. Irenaeus, *Against Heresies*, II, 34, 3, in ANF 1:411b–412a: "But he who shall ... prove himself ungrateful to his Maker, inasmuch as he has been created, and has not recognised Him who bestowed the gift upon him, deprives himself of the privilege of continuance for ever and ever."

precisely this reason, however, this redemption is not a magical device, not a wonder drug that one would just have to take in order to be "high" forever, so to speak; it is, as we already established at the beginning, not the renunciation of the adventure of being human but, rather, what makes it possible. Redemption is revealed only in accompaniment [*im Mitgehen*], and the more we entrust ourselves to it in faith and love, the more deeply and purely we become conscious of its truth.

III

Politics and Truth: Jesus before Pilate

Jesus' interrogation before the Sanhedrin had concluded in the way Caiaphas had expected: Jesus was found guilty of blasphemy, for which the penalty was death. But since only the Romans could carry out the death sentence, the case now had to be brought before Pilate and the political dimension of the guilty verdict had to be emphasized. Jesus had declared himself to be the Messiah; hence he had laid claim to the dignity of kingship, albeit in a way peculiarly his own. The claim to Messianic kingship was a political offense, one that had to be punished by Roman justice. With cockcrow, daybreak had arrived. The Roman governor used to hold court early in the morning.

So Jesus is now led by his accusers to the praetorium and is presented to Pilate as a criminal who deserves to die. It is the "day of preparation" for the Passover feast. The lambs are slaughtered in the afternoon for the evening meal. Hence cultic purity must be preserved; so the priestly accusers may not enter the Gentile praetorium, and they negotiate with the Roman governor outside the building.

From Joseph Ratzinger / Pope Benedict XVI, *Jesus von Nazareth: Zweiter Teil: Vom Einzug in Jerusalem bis zur Auferstehung* (Vatican City: Libreria Editrice Vaticana, 2011). Translated by Philip J. Whitmore as *Jesus of Nazareth: Holy Week: From the Entrance into Jerusalem to the Resurrection* (San Francisco: Ignatius Press, 2011), 183–202.

John, who provides this detail (18:28–29), thereby highlights the contradiction between the scrupulous attitude toward regulations for cultic purity and the question of real inner purity: it simply does not occur to Jesus' accusers that impurity does not come from entering a Gentile house but, rather, from the inner disposition of the heart. At the same time, the evangelist emphasizes that the Passover meal had not yet taken place and that the slaughter of the lambs was still to come.

In all essentials, the four Gospels harmonize with one another in their accounts of the progress of the trial. Only John reports the conversation between Jesus and Pilate, in which the question about Jesus' kingship, the reason for his death, is explored in depth (18:33–38). The historicity of this tradition is of course contested by exegetes. While Charles H. Dodd and Raymond E. Brown judge it positively, Charles K. Barrett is extremely critical: "John's additions and alterations do not inspire confidence in his historical reliability."[1] Certainly no one would claim that John set out to provide anything resembling a transcript of the trial. Yet we may assume that he was able to explain with great precision the core question at issue and that he presents us with a true account of the trial. Barrett also says that "John has with keen insight picked out the key of the Passion narrative in the kingship of Jesus, and has made its meaning clearer, perhaps, than any other New Testament writer".[2]

Now we must ask: Who exactly were Jesus' accusers? Who insisted that he be condemned to death? We must take note of the different answers that the Gospels give to

---

[1] Charles K. Barrett, *The Gospel according to St. John*, 2nd ed. (London: SPCK, 1978), 530.
[2] Ibid., 531.

this question. According to John, it was simply "the Jews". But John's use of this expression does not in any way indicate—as the modern reader might suppose—the people of Israel in general, even less is it "racist" in character. After all, John himself was ethnically a Jew, as were Jesus and all his followers. The entire early Christian community was made up of Jews. In John's Gospel, this word has a precise and clearly defined meaning: he is referring to the Temple aristocracy. So the circle of accusers who instigate Jesus' death is precisely indicated in the Fourth Gospel and clearly limited: it is the Temple aristocracy—and not without certain exceptions, as the reference to Nicodemus (7:50–52) shows.

In Mark's Gospel, the circle of accusers is broadened in the context of the Passover amnesty (Barabbas or Jesus): the *ochlos* enters the scene and opts for the release of Barabbas. *Ochlos* in the first instance simply means a crowd of people, the "masses". The word frequently has a pejorative connotation, meaning "mob". In any event, it does not refer to the Jewish people as such. In the case of the Passover amnesty (which admittedly is not attested in other sources, but even so need not be doubted), the people, as so often with such amnesties, have a right to put forward a proposal, expressed by way of "acclamation". Popular acclamation in this case has juridical character.[3] Effectively this "crowd" is made up of the followers of Barabbas who have been mobilized to secure the amnesty for him: as a rebel against Roman power, he could naturally count on a good number of supporters. So the Barabbas party, the "crowd", was conspicuous, while the followers of Jesus remained hidden out of fear; this meant that the *vox*

---

[3] Cf. Rudolf Pesch, *Das Markusevangelium*, vol. 2 (Freiburg: Herder, 1977), 466.

populi, on which Roman law was built, was represented one-sidedly. In Mark's account, then, in addition to "the Jews", that is to say, the dominant priestly circle, the *ochlos* comes into play, the circle of Barabbas' supporters, but not the Jewish people as such.

An extension of Mark's *ochlos,* with fateful consequences, is found in Matthew's account (27:25), which speaks of "all the people" and attributes to them the demand for Jesus' crucifixion. Matthew is certainly not recounting historical fact here: How could the whole people have been present at this moment to clamor for Jesus' death? It seems obvious that the historical reality is correctly described in John's account and in Mark's. The real group of accusers are the current Temple authorities, joined in the context of the Passover amnesty by the "crowd" of Barabbas' supporters. Here we may agree with Joachim Gnilka, who argues that Matthew, going beyond historical considerations, is attempting a theological etiology with which to account for the terrible fate of the people of Israel in the Jewish War, when land, city, and Temple were taken from them.[4] Matthew is thinking here of Jesus' prophecy concerning the end of the Temple: "O Jerusalem, Jerusalem, killing the prophets and stoning those who are sent to you! How often would I have gathered your children together as a hen gathers her brood under her wings, and you would not! Behold, your house is forsaken" (Mt 23:37–38).[5]

These words—as argued earlier, in the chapter on Jesus' eschatological discourse—remind us of the inner similarity between the prophet Jeremiah's message and that of Jesus. Jeremiah—against the blindness of the then dominant

---

[4] Cf. Joachim Gnilka, *Das Matthäusevangelium,* vol. 2 (Freiburg: Herder, 1988), 459.
[5] Cf. ibid., the whole of the section entitled "Gerichtsworte", 2:295–308.

circles—prophesied the destruction of the Temple and Israel's exile. But he also spoke of a "new covenant": punishment is not the last word; it leads to healing. In the same way, Jesus prophesies the "deserted house" and proceeds to offer the New Covenant "in his blood": ultimately it is a question of healing, not of destruction and rejection.

When in Matthew's account, the "whole people" say: "His blood be on us and on our children" (27:25), the Christian will remember that Jesus' blood speaks a different language from the blood of Abel (Heb 12:24): it does not cry out for vengeance and punishment; it brings reconciliation. It is not poured out *against* anyone; it is poured out *for* many, for all. "All have sinned and fall short of the glory of God ... *God* put [Jesus] forward as an expiation by his blood" (Rom 3:23, 25). Just as Caiaphas' words about the need for Jesus' death have to be read in an entirely new light from the perspective of faith, the same applies to Matthew's reference to blood: read in the light of faith, it means that we all stand in need of the purifying power of love that is his blood. These words are not a curse but, rather, redemption, salvation. Only when understood in terms of the theology of the Last Supper and the Cross, drawn from the whole of the New Testament, does this verse from Matthew's Gospel take on its correct meaning.

Let us move now from the accusers to the judge: the Roman governor Pontius Pilate. While Flavius Josephus and especially Philo of Alexandria paint a rather negative picture of him, other sources portray him as decisive, pragmatic, and realistic. It is often said that the Gospels presented him in an increasingly positive light out of a politically motivated pro-Roman tendency and that they shifted the blame for Jesus' death more and more onto the Jews. Yet there were no grounds for any such tendency in the historical circumstances of the evangelists: by the time the Gospels were written, Nero's persecution had already revealed the cruel side of the Roman state and the great arbitrariness of imperial power. If we may date the Book of Revelation to approximately the same period as John's Gospel, then it is clear that the Fourth Gospel did not come to be written in a context that could have given rise to a pro-Roman stance.

The image of Pilate in the Gospels presents the Roman prefect quite realistically as a man who could be brutal when he judged this to be in the interests of public order. Yet he also knew that Rome owed its world dominance not least to its tolerance of foreign divinities and to the capacity of Roman law to build peace. This is how he comes across to us during Jesus' trial.

The charge that Jesus claimed to be king of the Jews was a serious one. Rome had no difficulty in recognizing regional kings like Herod, but they had to be legitimated by Rome and they had to receive from Rome the definition and limitation of their sovereignty. A king without such legitimation was a rebel who threatened the *Pax Romana* and therefore had to be put to death.

Pilate knew, however, that no rebel uprising had been instigated by Jesus. Everything he had heard must have made Jesus seem to him like a religious fanatic, who may have offended against some Jewish legal and religious rulings, but that was of no concern to him. The Jews themselves would have to judge that. From the point of view of the Roman juridical and political order, which fell under his competence, there was nothing serious to hold against Jesus.

At this point we must pass from considerations about the person of Pilate to the trial itself. In John 18:34–35, it is clearly stated that, on the basis of the information in his possession, Pilate had nothing that would incriminate

Jesus. Nothing had come to the knowledge of the Roman authority that could in any way have posed a risk to law and order. The charge came from Jesus' own people, from the Temple authority. It must have astonished Pilate that Jesus' own people presented themselves to him as defenders of Rome, when the information at his disposal did not suggest the need for any action on his part.

Yet during the interrogation, we suddenly arrive at a dramatic moment: Jesus' confession. To Pilate's question: "So you are a king?" he answers: "You say that I am a king. For this I was born, and for this I have come into the world, to bear witness to the truth. Every one who is of the truth hears my voice" (Jn 18:37). Previously Jesus had said: "My kingship is not of this world; if my kingship were of this world, my servants would fight, that I might not be handed over to the Jews; but my kingship is not from the world" (18:36).

This "confession" of Jesus places Pilate in an extraordinary situation: the accused claims kingship and a kingdom (*basileía*). Yet he underlines the complete otherness of his kingship, and he even makes the particular point that must have been decisive for the Roman judge: no one is fighting for this kingship. If power, indeed military power, is characteristic of kingship and kingdoms, there is no sign of it in Jesus' case. And neither is there any threat to Roman order. This kingdom is powerless. It has "no legions".

With these words, Jesus created a thoroughly new concept of kingship and kingdom, and he held it up to Pilate, the representative of classical worldly power. What is Pilate to make of it, and what are we to make of it, this concept of kingdom and kingship? Is it unreal, is it sheer fantasy that can be safely ignored? Or does it somehow affect us? In addition to the clear delimitation of his concept of kingdom (no fighting, earthly powerlessness),

Jesus had introduced a positive idea, in order to explain the nature and particular character of the power of this kingship: namely, truth. Pilate brought another idea into play as the dialogue proceeded, one that came from his own world and was normally connected with "kingdom": namely, power—authority (*exousía*). Dominion demands power; it even defines it. Jesus, however, defines as the essence of his kingship witness to the truth. Is truth a political category? Or has Jesus' "kingdom" nothing to do with politics? To which order does it belong? If Jesus bases his concept of kingship and kingdom on truth as the fundamental category, then it is entirely understandable that the pragmatic Pilate asks him: "What is truth?" (18:38).

It is the question that is also asked by modern political theory: Can politics accept truth as a structural category? Or must truth, as something unattainable, be relegated to the subjective sphere, its place taken by an attempt to build peace and justice using whatever instruments are available to power? By relying on truth, does not politics, in view of the impossibility of attaining consensus on truth, make itself a tool of particular traditions that in reality are merely forms of holding on to power?

And yet, on the other hand, what happens when truth counts for nothing? What kind of justice is then possible? Must there not be common criteria that guarantee real justice for all—criteria that are independent of the arbitrariness of changing opinions and powerful lobbies? Is it not true that the great dictatorships were fed by the power of the ideological lie and that only truth was capable of bringing freedom?

What is truth? The pragmatist's question, tossed off with a degree of skepticism, is a very serious question, bound up with the fate of mankind. What, then, is truth? Are we able to recognize it? Can it serve as a criterion for our intellect and will, both in individual choices and in the life of the community?

The classic definition from scholastic philosophy designates truth as "adaequatio intellectus et rei" (conformity between the intellect and reality).[6] If a man's intellect reflects a thing as it is in itself, then he has found truth: but only a small fragment of reality—not truth in its grandeur and integrity. We come closer to what Jesus meant with another of Saint Thomas' teachings: "Truth is in God's intellect properly and firstly (*proprie et primo*); in human intellect, it is present properly and derivatively (*proprie quidem et secundario*)."[7] And in conclusion, we arrive at the succinct formula: God is "ipsa summa et prima veritas" (truth itself, the sovereign and first truth).[8]

This formula brings us close to what Jesus means when he speaks of the truth, when he says that his purpose in coming into the world was to "bear witness to the truth". Again and again in the world, truth and error, truth and untruth, are almost inseparably mixed together. *The* truth in all its grandeur and purity does not appear. The world is "true" to the extent that it reflects God: the creative logic, the eternal reason that brought it to birth. And it becomes more and more true the closer it draws to God. Man becomes true, he becomes himself, when he grows in God's likeness. Then he attains to his proper nature. God is the reality that gives being and intelligibility.

"Bearing witness to the truth" means giving priority to God and to his will over against the interests of the world and its powers. God is the criterion of being. In this sense, truth is the real "king" that confers light and greatness

---

[6] Thomas Aquinas, *Summa Theologiae* I, q. 21, a. 2c.
[7] Thomas Aquinas, *De Verit.*, q. 1, a. 4c.
[8] Thomas Aquinas, *Summa Theologiae* I, q. 16, a. 5c.

upon all things. We may also say that bearing witness to the truth means making creation intelligible and its truth accessible from God's perspective—the perspective of creative reason—in such a way that it can serve as a criterion and a signpost in this world of ours, in such a way that the great and the mighty are exposed to the power of truth, the common law, the law of truth.

Let us say plainly: the unredeemed state of the world consists precisely in the failure to understand the meaning of creation, in the failure to recognize truth; as a result, the rule of pragmatism is imposed, by which the strong arm of the powerful becomes the god of this world.

At this point, modern man is tempted to say: Creation has become intelligible to us through science. Indeed, Francis S. Collins, for example, who led the Human Genome Project, says with joyful astonishment: "The language of God was revealed."[9] Indeed, in the magnificent mathematics of creation, which today we can read in the human genetic code, we recognize the language of God. But unfortunately not the whole language. The functional truth about man has been discovered. But the truth about man himself—who he is, where he comes from, what he should do, what is right, what is wrong—this unfortunately cannot be read in the same way. Hand in hand with growing knowledge of functional truth there seems to be an increasing blindness toward "truth" itself—toward the question of our real identity and purpose.

What is truth? Pilate was not alone in dismissing this question as unanswerable and irrelevant for his purposes. Today too, in political argument and in discussion of the foundations of law, it is generally experienced as disturbing.

---

[9] Francis S. Collins, *The Language of God: A Scientist Presents Evidence for Belief* (New York: Free Press, 2006), 122.

Yet if man lives without truth, life passes him by; ultimately he surrenders the field to whoever is the stronger. "Redemption" in the fullest sense can only consist in the truth becoming recognizable. And it becomes recognizable when God becomes recognizable. He becomes recognizable in Jesus Christ. In Christ, God entered the world and set up the criterion of truth in the midst of history. Truth is outwardly powerless in the world, just as Christ is powerless by the world's standards: he has no legions; he is crucified. Yet in his very powerlessness, he is powerful: only thus, again and again, does truth become power.

In the dialogue between Jesus and Pilate, the subject matter is Jesus' kingship and, hence, the kingship, the "kingdom", of God. In the course of this same conversation, it becomes abundantly clear that there is no discontinuity between Jesus' Galilean teaching—the proclamation of the kingdom of God—and his Jerusalem teaching. The center of the message, all the way to the Cross—all the way to the inscription above the Cross—is the Kingdom of God, the new kingship represented by Jesus. And this kingship is centered on truth. The kingship proclaimed by Jesus, at first in parables and then at the end quite openly before the earthly judge, is none other than the kingship of truth. The inauguration of this kingship is man's true liberation.

At the same time, it becomes clear that between the pre-Resurrection focus on the Kingdom of God and the post-Resurrection focus on faith in Jesus Christ as Son of God there is no contradiction. In Christ, God— the Truth—entered the world. Christology is the concrete form acquired by the proclamation of God's kingdom.

After the interrogation, Pilate knew for certain what in principle he had already known beforehand: this Jesus was no political rebel; his message and his activity posed no threat for the Roman rulers. Whether Jesus had offended against the Torah was of no concern to him as a Roman. Yet Pilate seems also to have experienced a certain superstitious wariness concerning this remarkable figure. True, Pilate was a skeptic. As a man of his time, though, he did not exclude the possibility that gods or, at any rate, god-like beings could take on human form. John tells us that "the Jews" accused Jesus of making himself the Son of God, and then he adds: "When Pilate heard these words, he was even more afraid" (19:8).

I think we must take seriously the idea of Pilate's fear: Perhaps there really was something divine in this man? Perhaps Pilate would be opposing divine power if he were to condemn him? Perhaps he would have to reckon with the anger of the deity? I think his attitude during the trial can be explained not only on the basis of a certain commitment to see justice done, but also on the basis of such considerations as these.

Jesus' accusers obviously realize this, and so they now play off one fear against another. Against the superstitious fear of a possible divine presence, they appeal to the entirely practical fear of forfeiting the emperor's favor, being removed from office, and thus plunging into a downward spiral. The declaration: "If you release this man, you are not Caesar's friend" (Jn 19:12) is a threat. In the end, concern for career proves stronger than fear of divine powers.

Before the final verdict, though, there is a further dramatic and painful interlude in three acts, which we must consider at least briefly.

The first act sees Pilate presenting Jesus as a candidate for the Passover amnesty and seeking in this way to release him. In doing so, he puts himself in a fatal situation. Anyone put forward as a candidate for the amnesty is in principle already condemned. Otherwise, the amnesty would make no sense. If the crowd has the right of acclamation, then, according to their response, the one they do *not* choose is to be regarded as condemned. In this sense, the proposed release on the basis of the amnesty already tacitly implies condemnation.

Regarding the juxtaposition of Jesus and Barabbas and the theological significance of the choice placed before the crowd, I have already written in some detail in Part One of this book (pp. 40–41). Here I shall merely recall the essentials. According to our translations, John refers to Barabbas simply as a robber (18:40). In the political context of the time, though, the Greek word that John uses had also acquired the meaning of terrorist or freedom fighter. It is clear from Mark's account that this is the intended meaning: "And among the rebels in prison, who had committed murder in the insurrection, there was a man called Barabbas" (15:7).

Barabbas ("Son of the Father") is a kind of Messianic figure. Two interpretations of Messianic hope are juxtaposed here in the offer of the Passover amnesty. In terms of Roman law, it is a case of two criminals convicted of the same offense—two rebels against the *Pax Romana*. It is clear that Pilate prefers the nonviolent "fanatic" that he sees in Jesus. Yet the crowd and the Temple authorities have different categories. If the Temple aristocracy felt constrained to declare: "We have no king but Caesar" (Jn 19:15), this only *appears* to be a renunciation of Israel's Messianic hope: "We do not want *this* king" is what they mean. They would like to see a different solution to the problem. Again and again, mankind will be faced with this same choice: to say yes to the God who works only through the power of truth and love, or to build on something tangible and concrete—on violence.

Jesus' followers are absent from the place of judgment, absent through fear. But they are also absent in the sense that they fail to step forward *en masse*. Their voice will make itself heard on the day of Pentecost in Peter's preaching, which cuts "to the heart" the very people who had earlier supported Barabbas. In answer to the question "Brethren, what shall we do?" they receive the answer: "Repent"—renew and transform your thinking, your being (cf. Acts 2:37–38). This is the summons that, in view of the Barabbas scene and its many recurrences throughout history, should tear open our hearts and change our lives.

The second act is succinctly summarized by John as follows: "Then Pilate took Jesus and scourged him" (19:1). In Roman criminal law, scourging was the punishment that accompanied the death sentence.[10] In John's Gospel, however, it is presented as an act during the interrogation, a measure that the prefect was empowered to take on the basis of his responsibility for law enforcement. It was an extremely barbaric punishment; the victim was "struck by several torturers for as long as it took for them to grow tired, and for the flesh of the criminal to hang down in bleeding shreds".[11] Rudolf Pesch notes in this regard: "The fact that Simon of Cyrene has to carry the cross-beam for Jesus and that Jesus dies so quickly may well be attributable to the torture of scourging, during which other criminals sometimes would already have died."[12]

The third act is the crowning with thorns. The soldiers are playing cruel games with Jesus. They know that he claims to be a king. But now he is in their hands; now it pleases them to humiliate him, to display their power over him, and perhaps to offload vicariously onto him their

---

[10] Martin Hengel and Anna Maria Schwemer, *Jesus und das Judentum* (Tübingen: Mohr Siebeck, 2007), 609.

[11] Josef Blinzler, *Der Prozess Jesu*, 4th ed. (Regensburg: Pustet,1969), 321.

[12] Pesch, *Markusevangelium* 2:467.

anger against their rulers. Him whose whole body is torn and wounded, they vest, as a caricature, with the tokens of imperial majesty: the purple robe, the crown plaited from thorns, and the reed scepter. They pay homage to him: "Hail, King of the Jews"; their homage consists of blows to his head, through which they once more express their utter contempt for him (Mt 27:28–30; Mk 15:17–19; Jn 19:2–3).

The history of religions knows the figure of the mock king—related to the figure of the "scapegoat". Whatever may be afflicting the people is offloaded onto him: in this way it is to be driven out of the world. Without realizing it, the soldiers were actually accomplishing what those rites and ceremonies were unable to achieve: "Upon him was the chastisement that made us whole, and with his stripes we are healed" (Is 53:5). Thus caricatured, Jesus is led to Pilate, and Pilate presents him to the crowd—to all mankind: "Ecce homo", "Here is the man!" (Jn 19:5). The Roman judge is no doubt distressed at the sight of the wounded and derided figure of this mysterious defendant. He is counting on the compassion of those who see him.

"Ecce homo"—the expression spontaneously takes on a depth of meaning that reaches far beyond this moment in history. In Jesus, it is man himself that is manifested. In him is displayed the suffering of all who are subjected to violence, all the downtrodden. His suffering mirrors the inhumanity of worldly power, which so ruthlessly crushes the powerless. In him is reflected what we call "sin": this is what happens when man turns his back upon God and takes control over the world into his own hands. There is another side to all this, though: Jesus' innermost dignity cannot be taken from him. The hidden God remains present within him. Even the man subjected to violence and vilification remains the image of God.

Ever since Jesus submitted to violence, it has been the wounded, the victims of violence, who have been the image of the God who chose to suffer for us. So Jesus in the throes of his Passion is an image of hope: God is on the side of those who suffer.

Finally, Pilate takes his place on the judgment seat. Once again he says: "Here is your King!" (Jn 19:14). Then he pronounces the death sentence.

Indeed, the great "Truth" of which Jesus had spoken was inaccessible to Pilate. Yet the concrete truth of this particular case he knew very well. He knew that this Jesus was not a political criminal and that the kingship he claimed did not represent any political danger—that he ought therefore to be acquitted.

As prefect, Pilate represented Roman law, on which the *Pax Romana* rested—the peace of the empire that spanned the world. This peace was secured, on the one hand, through Rome's military might. But military force alone does not generate peace. Peace depends on justice. Rome's real strength lay in its legal system, the juridical order on which men could rely. Pilate—let us repeat— knew the truth of this case, and hence he knew what justice demanded of him.

Yet ultimately it was the pragmatic concept of law that won the day with him: more important than the truth of this case, he probably reasoned, is the peace-building role of law, and in this way he doubtless justified his action to himself. Releasing this innocent man could not only cause him personal damage—and such fear was certainly a decisive factor behind his action—it could also give rise to further disturbances and unrest, which had to be avoided at all costs, especially at the time of the Passover. In this case peace counted for more than justice in Pilate's eyes. Not only the great, inaccessible Truth but also the concrete truth of Jesus' case had to recede into the background: in this way he believed he was fulfilling the real purpose of the law—its peace-building function. Perhaps this was how he eased his conscience. For the time being, all seemed to be going well. Jerusalem remained calm. At a later date, though, it would become clear that peace, in the final analysis, cannot be established at the expense of truth.

IV

Augustine's Confrontation with the Political Theology of Rome

1. THE REJECTION OF ROME'S POLITICAL THEOLOGY

As in the case of Origen, Augustine's point of departure for a political theology was polemical. The fall of Rome in 410 had, once again, elicited a pagan reaction. "Where were the graves of the apostles?" was the outcry. They had obviously been unable to protect Rome, the city that was unconquered the entire time that it had entrusted itself to the protection of its local gods. Rome's defeat was conspicuous proof that the Creator God whom Christian faith revered had no interest in political happenings. This God might well be concerned with man's eternal happiness, but events had demonstrated—even vividly—that he was unconcerned with the political realm. The domain of politics clearly had its own set of laws, which had no bearing on the supreme God; hence it should have its own religion as well.[1]

From Joseph Ratzinger, *Die Einheit der Nationen: Eine Vision der Kirchenväter* (Salzburg: Pustet, 1962); translated by Boniface Ramsey as *The Unity of the Nations: A Vision of the Church Fathers* (Washington, D.C.: Catholic University of America Press, 2015), 69–113.

[1] See Augustine, *The City of God* I–V, which deals at great length with what is only briefly sketched out here.

What the masses demanded more out of a general feeling, that in addition to the main religion there also had to be a religion for this-worldly and especially for political things, could be given a much deeper underpinning based on antiquity's philosophical convictions. One need only recall the Platonic axiom formulated by Apuleius: "Between God and man there is no contact."[2] Platonism was utterly convinced of the infinite gulf between God and the world, spirit and matter. God's direct dealing with the things of the world would necessarily have appeared to it as completely impossible. God's responsibility for the world was met by intermediate beings to which a person would have to have recourse when it was a matter of the things of this world.[3] In this exaggerated concept of God's transcendence, according to which he was removed from the world and cut off from the concrete activities associated with human life, Augustine rightly observed the seed of a revolt against the all-embracing claims of Christian faith, which could never tolerate the exclusion of the political from the providence of the one God. In the face of the pagan reaction, which aimed at reinstituting the religious status of the this-worldly *polis* and, along with that, relegating the Christian religion (which looked forward to the next world) to the private sphere, Augustine began by making two fundamental assertions.

a. The Untruthfulness of the Political Religion

His first assertion was that the political "religion" of Rome had no truth in it. It was built upon the canonization of

---

[2] *On the God of Socrates* 4, cited in *City of God* IX, 16.
[3] See *City of God* VIII–IX.

custom as opposed to truth.[4] This rejection of the truth, or rather this stand against the truth for the sake of custom, was frequently espoused by the representatives of Roman religion themselves—Scaevola, Varro, Seneca.[5] What was

[4] See ibid., IV, 31, where Augustine says of the Roman polymath Varro: "It might seem that I am guessing here, except for the fact that Varro himself states quite openly in another place, where he is speaking of religious rites, that there are many things that are true which it is not useful for the common people to know, and many also which, even if false, it is expedient for the populace to think true.... The malignant demons take great delight in this deception, for it means that they have both the deceivers and the deceived in their possession" (trans. W. Babcock, *The Works of Saint Augustine* I, 6, and I, 7 [Hyde Park, N.Y., 2012–13], I, 139). Shortly before, at IV, 30, he had said of the Spanish Stoic philosopher Quintus Lucilius Balbus: "As anyone can see, he is trying hard, out of respect for the city's established customs, to praise the religion of his ancestors and wants desperately to separate it out from superstition, but he can find no way to do this" (Babcock, *Augustine* I, 138). At VI, 4, he speaks again of Varro: "He has admitted that, when he wrote his books on divine matters, he was not writing about the truth that belongs to nature but about the falsehood that belongs to error. As I mentioned in the fourth book [of *The City of God*], he has stated this more clearly elsewhere. For he said that, if he were himself founding a new city, he would have written in accord with the rule of nature, but since he found himself situated in an already-established city, he could do nothing but follow its customs" (Babcock, *Augustine* I, 190). One cannot help but recall Tertullian's magnificent statement in *On the Veiling of Virgins* 1 that Christ referred to himself, not as the custom, but as the truth. See J. N. Bakhuizen van den Brink, "Traditio im theologischen Sinn", *Vigiliae Christianae* 13 (1959): 65–86.

[5] In addition to the texts of Varro already cited in the previous note, see also *City of God* IV, 31: "Those who first set up images of the gods for the people both reduced reverence and increased error in their cities" (Babcock, *Augustine* I, 140); and likewise ibid., IV, 9. On Scaevola, see ibid., IV, 27: "It is recorded that the pontiff Scaevola, whose literary knowledge was immense, argued that three views of the gods are passed down to us: one by the poets, another by the philosophers, and a third by political leaders. The first, he says, is mere nonsense, because many disgraceful tales have been made up about the gods, and the second is not suitable for civic society, because some things it contains are superfluous and some are even harmful for the people to know. The superfluous matters are no great issue, for, as the commonplace among jurists goes, 'Superfluous things do no harm.' But what are the points that actually do harm when they are made known to the multitude? They are, he says, such statements as these: 'That Hercules, Aesculapius, Castor, and Pollux are not gods, for the learned claim that these were men who passed beyond our human

contrary to the truth was acceptable for the sake of tradition. Concern for the *polis* and its well-being justified the violation of truth. In other words, the well-being of the state, which was believed to be dependent on the continuance of its ancient forms, was more highly valued than the truth.

It was here that Augustine saw one of the great distinctions between Rome and Christianity in all its acuity: in the Roman understanding, religion was an institution of the state and, hence, a function of the state; as such, it was subordinate to the state. It was not an absolute that was independent of the interests of the various groups that professed it; rather, its value was dependent on its serviceability vis-à-vis the state, which was the absolute. In the Christian understanding, on the other hand, religion had to do, not with custom, but with truth, which was absolute. It was, therefore, not instituted by the state but, rather, had itself instituted a new community that embraced everyone who lived in God's truth.[6] From

---

condition.' What else? 'That cities do not have true images of the gods, for the true god has neither sex nor age nor defined body parts.' The pontiff does not want the people to know these things because, in fact, he does not consider them to be false. Clearly, then, his view is that it is expedient for cities to be deceived in matters of religion" (Babcock, *Augustine* I, 134–35). Augustine cites Seneca's position vis-à-vis the cult of the state, ibid., VI, 10: "The wise man will observe all these rites not because they are pleasing to the gods but because they are enjoined by law"; and a few lines later: "As for all that ignoble throng of gods assembled through the ages by ancient superstition, we will adore them, but only with the reminder that their worship has far more to do with custom than with truth" (Babcock, *Augustine* I, 204). The citations from Seneca are taken from a lost work entitled *On Superstition*. On Augustine's relationship to Seneca, see *Bibliothèque Augustinienne* 34, 571–72. On the official cult and interior religion, see ibid., 572–74, with numerous references to Cicero.

[6] See *City of God* VI, 4: "Varro himself states that he wrote first about human matters and only then about divine matters, because cities came into existence first, and then these rites were instituted by them. The true religion, however, was not instituted by any earthly city; instead, clearly, the true religion itself instituted the heavenly city" (Babcock, *Augustine* I, 190).

that perspective, Augustine understood the Christian faith as a freeing—namely, a freeing from the tyranny of custom for the sake of the truth.[7]

b. The Power of the Demons

The political religion of the Romans, to be sure, did not possess any truth, but there was a truth that hovered over it, and this truth was that the enslavement of man to untruthful customs had delivered him over to the ungodly powers that the Christian faith called demons; to that degree, the worship of idols was not merely a foolish and baseless affectation but, in its delivering over of man to the renunciation of truth, had become the worship of demons. This was Augustine's second fundamental assertion.

Behind the ineffectual gods stood the highly effectual power of the demons,[8] and behind the enslavement to custom stood enslavement to evil spirits. Herein lay the true depth of Christian freeing and the freedom that had been gained in it. Inasmuch as this freedom set a person free from custom, it freed him from a power that man had in fact himself created but that long before had outgrown him and now lorded it over him, a power that had turned into an objective power that was independent

---

[7] See ibid., IV, 30: "Let us Christians, therefore, give thanks to the Lord our God ... who, through the supreme humility of Christ ... and through the faith of the martyrs who died for the truth and now live with the truth, has overthrown these superstitions by the free service of his people ... not only in the hearts of the religious but also in the very temples of the superstitious" (Babcock, *Augustine* I, 139). Ibid., VI, 2: "What should we make of this, except that a man of the greatest acumen and learning [i.e., Varro] (although not set free by the Holy Spirit) was obliged to submit to the laws and customs of his city!" (Babcock, *Augustine* I, 188, alt.).

[8] This affirmation can be found throughout the first part of *City of God*. What follows is a nonexhaustive selection of texts: IV, 1, 27, 29, 31; V, 12,18, 24; VI, 4; VIII, 14 (fundamental), 18; IX, 3, 8–9.

of him, into an opening for the power of evil as such that was overwhelming him, which was called "demons". Being freed from custom for the sake of the truth meant being freed from the power of the demons that hid behind custom.[9] At this point, the sacrifice of Christ and of Christians now became truly understandable as redemption—in other words, as a setting free. It overthrew the political cult that was opposed to truth and replaced the political cult, which was a cult of demons, with the one universal service of the truth, which was freedom.[10]

Here Augustine's thinking coincides with that of Origen. Just as Origen had understood the religious absolutizing of national identity as the work of the demonic angels of the peoples, and the supranational unity of Christians as the being set free from the prison of "the people", so Augustine viewed the political from the perspective of antiquity—namely, as the divinization of the *polis*, albeit in the sense of its demonization—and saw in Christianity the overcoming of the demonic power of the political, which had suppressed the truth. For him, likewise, the

---

[9] See ibid., IV, 31: "How vast and how malign the power of the demons is—the power from which we are set free by the unique sacrifice of the holy blood shed for us and the gift of the Spirit bestowed on us" (Babcock, *Augustine* I, 140). Ibid., V, 18: "If a father [i.e., the Roman Junius Brutus, who opposed King Tarquin] could kill his sons for the sake of liberty for men who were going to die in any case, and for the sake of desire for the praises that we gain from mortal men, is it any great thing if, for the sake of the true liberty which sets us free from the dominion of iniquity and death and the devil, we do not kill our sons but simply count Christ's poor among our sons? It is not from desire for human praise that we do this but from love of setting people free—free not from a King Tarquin but from the demons and from the prince of demons" (Babcock, *Augustine* I, 167–68). Ibid., IX, 15: "on those whose hearts he purifies by faith and has delivered from their foul dominion" (Babcock, *Augustine* I, 293).

[10] See Ratzinger, *Volk und Haus Gottes in Augustins Lehre von der Kirche*, 188–234.

pagan gods were not mere illusions but the fantastic masks behind which real powers and forces were hidden, which denied man access to absolute values by enclosing him in relativity, and the domain of the political was the actual domain of these powers. Augustine certainly allowed for the truth of Euhemerus' idea—that all the gods were originally once human beings and that hence the whole of pagan religion was founded on an exaggeration of human worth—while at the same time seeing that this idea by no means solved the riddle of the pagan religions. The powers that people apparently thought came from within themselves soon showed themselves to be objective forces, or demons, that exercised a very real domination over them.[11] Only God himself, the power over all powers, could free human beings from them.[12]

2. THE STARTING POINT FOR THE AUGUSTINIAN THEOLOGY OF THE POLITICAL

A question remains as to what positive theology of the political Augustine can offer after so many negative statements. Here as well, his reflections were developed over against the two most important political philosophies of his time, Stoicism and Platonism.

---

[11] Augustine touches briefly on the problem of euhemerism in connection with the theses of Scaevola in *City of God* IV, 27. There is a more extended treatment (with a reference to Euhemerus), ibid., VI, 7; and an especially detailed one in connection with Hermes Trismegistos, ibid., VIII, 26. In all these instances, his explanations fall back on the idea of the demonic. See also *Bibliothèque Augustinienne* 33, 785; 34, 585–86.

[12] On the concept of freedom, or liberation, see nn. 7 and 9 in this chapter. See further the debate with Porphyry on the concept of purification in *City of God* X, 24–32, well summarized at 32: "This is the religion that contains the universal way of the soul's liberation, for no soul can be liberated by any other way" (Babcock, *Augustine* I, 344).

a. The Antithesis of the Stoa

Stoic monism had allowed for the whole world to be viewed as saturated with divinity and, correspondingly, for the places where its power was especially concentrated to be given the qualifier "divine". Understandably, the political theology of the Romans seized hold of this particular concept (from which it very quickly derived the right of the state) in order to identify itself as the norm and source of religion.[13] Augustine set his Christian faith in creation over against the monism of the Stoa: "In the true theology, the earth is the work of God, not his mother."[14] The world contained in itself nothing absolute. It was entirely God's creation and his work; the absolute was beyond it, not in it.

b. The Antithesis of Platonism

If Stoicism meant the mingling of God and the world and thus the abolition of transcendence, Platonism, on the contrary, was marked by a radical exaggeration of transcendence: God had nothing to do with the world.[15] For Augustine, who believed in the incarnation of God, this dogma was untenable. God made the world, and it only

---

[13] Consequently it is understandable that Varro, in his search for a philosophical basis, found it in Stoicism. Augustine features his definition of the concept of God, ibid., IV, 31. On the origins and effect of his threefold concept of theology, which was analyzed in depth by Augustine, see J. Pépin, "La 'théologie tripartite' de Varron: Essai de reconstitution et recherche de sources", *Revue des Études Augustiniennes* 2 (1956): 265–94. See also *Bibliothèque Augustinienne* 33, 813; 34, 565. Pépin, "La 'théologie tripartite'", 269–78, offers a fine analysis of the extant writings of Scaevola.

[14] *City of God* VI, 8 (Babcock, *Augustine* I, 197, alt.).

[15] See n. 2 of this chapter. For an extensive discussion, see *Bibliothèque Augustinienne* 34, 612–14.

existed by reason of the fact that he attended to it. No worldly material was contaminated, and no creature was unworthy of God or able to reach him only through intermediaries. The only contaminated thing was a mind turned against God, and alienation from God came from a spiritual rejection of him.[16] The foundational Platonic dogma, "Between God and man there is no contact",[17] was for Augustine replaced by the objective fact, witnessed to by Christian faith, that God had become man.[18] God, who had created the world, also remained its Lord; the Creator God was also the God of history. From this realization sprang the leitmotiv of Augustine's political theology: *Ipse dat regna terrena.*[19] It is God himself who distributes earthly kingdoms. The political world, with its manifold and opposing states, had no special divinities but, rather, was subordinate to the one God, whose works were creation and history.

---

[16] See *City of God* IX, 17, where Augustine conflates and slightly alters Plotinus, *Enneads* I, 6, 8; II, 3: "We must flee, therefore, to our beloved homeland. Our Father is there; all is there. What ship are we to use, then, what means of flight? We must become like God." To this Augustine adds: "If it is true that the more a person is like God, the closer he is to God, then the only way to be distant from God is to be unlike him." Particularly noteworthy is the statement at the end of the same chapter: "And meanwhile there are two matters of no small importance that he showed us, for our salvation, by his incarnation—that true divinity cannot be contaminated by the flesh, and that we should not think that the demons are superior to us just because they do not have flesh" (Babcock, *Augustine* I, 297).

[17] Ibid., IX 16, cited above in n. 2 of this chapter.

[18] In *Confessions* VIII, Augustine describes how an acknowledgment of the *descensus Dei*, the descent of God into our human condition, contributed to his going beyond Platonism. Over the course of his life, he saw there the real difference between Christianity and mere philosophizing. See Ratzinger, *Volk und Haus Gottes in Augustins Lehre von der Kirche*, 2–12.

[19] *City of God* IV, 33. See also ibid., V, l: "It is beyond doubt ... that human kingdoms are established by divine providence" (Babcock, *Augustine* I, 144). See *Bibliothèque Augustinienne* 33, 767–69.

3. THE THEOLOGICAL USE OF THE OLD TESTAMENT AND OF ROMAN HISTORY

What this meant concretely in terms of political classification became evident, on the one hand, with respect to the history of Rome and, on the other, with respect to that of Israel. Both histories were interconnected in the sense that only when both were viewed together would God's plan for the world be completely recognizable. The Old Testament at first set up an earthly rule, even though its meaning was spiritual; it included earthly promises and gifts. In fact, it was precisely this that was the "sacrament" of the Old Testament and its real salvation-historical meaning; for those who could grasp it, this "sacrament" pointed toward eternal goods, while at the same time it served as the means to make clear to everyone that even earthly goods were subject to God's disposal.[20] The earthly theocracy of the one God was established in Israel as a sign in world history, which indicated that there was no division between so-called high religion and political religion but, rather, that God's rule was one and that it encompassed all human beings and all areas of human existence.

This Old Testament message, however, was enlarged and expanded by the knowledge that was gained from the history of Rome. Here, of course, idolaters possessed a vast measure of earthly goods and earthly success. But it had to be that way. On the one hand, God had given his own people in Israel earthly rule in order to show that

---

[20] See *City of God* IV, 33: "And this is the sacrament of the Old Testament, where the New Testament was hidden—that, in the Old Testament, the promises and gifts are of earthly things, although even then spiritual men understood (but did not yet openly proclaim) both the eternity signified by those temporal things and which of God's gifts are the ones that bring true happiness" (Babcock, *Augustine* I, 141, alt.). The theme is continued, ibid., IV, 34. See also *Bibliothèque Augustinienne* 33, 814–17.

this, too, came from him. On the other, he had given
demon-worshippers—first in the great Eastern kingdoms
and then in Rome—earthly power in order to show that
none of this possessed any ultimate value but, rather, was
something entirely penultimate, which man had to out-
grow so as to arrive at his true goal. "The one true God
himself gives earthly kingdoms to the good and to the evil
alike.... As for [true] happiness, he gives this only to the
good. Slaves can have or not have happiness, and rulers
can have or not have happiness, although full happiness
will come only in the life where no one will be a slave
any longer. And the reason why God gives earthly kingdoms to the good and the evil alike is this: to keep his
worshippers, who are still no more advanced in mind than
little children, from yearning for this gift from him as if it
were some great thing."[21] Hence, earthly rule in the hands
of the good and the bad was the divine sign in history
with a double meaning that pointed both to God's absolute power and to the relativity of this-worldly values, and
especially of political entities.

The history of Rome as an earthly state in which the
history of the world was ultimately gathered up permitted
a deeper understanding of these facts. First, there was the
history of the Roman republic, which was able to push
its frontiers to the ends of the earth. Rome's good fortune in this respect gave greater exposure to the same dia-
lectic that lay behind every earthly institution. The basis
for Rome's success, in Augustine's eyes, was the *prisca virtus Romana*, ancient Roman virtue. But what really was
this Roman virtue? To use Virgil's definition, it consisted
in *amor patriae laudumque immensa cupido*, "love of country

---

[21] *City of God* IV, 33 (Babcock, *Augustine* I, 141). On the succession of kingdoms from East to West, see ibid., V, 13.

and immense desire for praise".[22] It was a renunciation of
other burdens for the sake of the one burden of bound-
less patriotic ambition and the will to power. Thus, the
Romans were good "within the context of the earthly
city"—good, in other words, if a nation's earthly greatness were taken to be the highest value.[23] Their virtue
represented a renunciation of many vices for the sake of
a single vice, namely, the absolutization of the nation.[24]
So it was only right that what they so ardently strove for
and were prepared to sacrifice everything for was actually
granted them: national greatness. But what was bestowed
on them by a just God was at the same time their punishment. They had made the nation's earthly greatness their

<hr>

[22] *Aeneid* VI, 823, cited in *City of God* V, 18.

[23] *City of God* V, 19 (Babcock, *Augustine* I, 172). See also ibid., V, 12: "We
can see what they wanted virtue to culminate in, and what the good among
them correlated virtue with, namely, honor.... Therefore virtue should not
follow on the glory, honor and power which the Romans desired for themselves and which the good among them strove to attain by 'good arts'.... For
there is no true virtue except the virtue that is directed toward the end where
man's good is actually found, the good than which there is no better" (Babcock, *Augustine* I, 161–62). *City of God* V, 13: "Nevertheless, it is for the better
that people who do not restrain their baser lusts by the pious faith and the love
of intelligible beauty that are given by the Holy Spirit at least do so by their
desire for human praise and glory. They certainly are not saints, but at least they
are less vile" (Babcock, *Augustine* I, 163).

[24] See *City of God* V, 13: "Who, for the sake of honor, praise and glory,
served the good of the country in which they sought their own glory and did
not hesitate to put its well-being above their own. For the sake of this one
vice—that is, the love of praise—these men suppressed the love of riches and
many other vices" (Babcock, *Augustine* I, 163). *City of God* V, 14: "But since
these Romans belonged to an earthly city, and since the goal set before them
in all their services on its behalf was to secure its safety and to gain a kingdom
not in heaven but on earth, not in eternal life but in a life where the dying pass
away and are succeeded by those who are going to die in turn, what else was
there for them to love but glory? And what glory but the glory by which they
yearned to find a life after death, as it were, on the lips of those who praised
them?" (Babcock, *Augustine* I, 165).

highest value and had thereby cut themselves off from
something greater, the values of eternity. They belonged
to those persons of whom the Lord said: "Truly, I say to
you, they have received their reward" (Mt 6:2).[25] They
had sought and obtained an earthly kingdom in place of an
eternal kingdom and earthly prominence in place of eternal
glory. The Roman Empire, the sign of its greatness, was
simultaneously the sign of their eternal rejection. That
was the sober judgment of the bishop of Hippo regarding the splendor that had blinded others' eyes. Rome
ultimately became a moral example for Augustine: the
immense effort that people had committed to the transitory goal of an earthly state and earthly greatness should
provide a powerful impetus for the believer to spend all his
energies on the eternal goal that had become visible and
accessible for him in the person of Christ Jesus.[26]

The republic was followed by the imperial age in
Rome, and that too had double significance, inasmuch as
it produced both a Nero and a Constantine. Nero himself, the epitome of everything horrible, had possessed
power over a world empire. "But even in the case of
men such as these, the power to dominate is given only
by the providence of the supreme God, when he judges
that the state of human affairs deserves such overlords."[27]
This was a powerful statement made by a man who had

[25] See *City of God* V, 15.

[26] There are wonderful applications of Roman virtue to Christian life, *City of God* V, 18. See E. von Ivanka, "Römische Ideologie in der 'Civitas Dei'", in Congrès International Augustinien, *Augustinus Magister* III (Paris, 1955), 411–17; *Bibliothèque Augustinienne* 33, 830–31.

[27] *City of God* V, 19 (Babcock, *Augustine* I, 172). Augustine adds to this two scriptural proofs: "By me kings reign, and by me tyrants hold the earth" (Prov 8:15), which he admits could be translated differently from the Latin version that he had before him, and so he cites a further text: "He causes the hypocrite to reign on account of the perversity of the people" (Job 34:30).

an unvarnished understanding of human wickedness and who spoke about it in an unvarnished way. And he who had previously always offered the *prisca virtus Romana* as the reason for Roman greatness added reflectively: "As best I could, then, I have explained why the one true and just God aided the Romans in obtaining the glory of such a great empire, for they were good men within the context of the earthly city. It is possible, of course, that there is another more hidden reason, better known to God than to us, which has to do with the diverse merits of humankind."[28] Who knows, Augustine seems to want to say, whether the Roman Empire throughout its history, and not merely the relatively brief moment when Nero ruled it, was perhaps God's scourge, from which we should turn away with a shudder instead of foolishly admiring?

Yet along with Nero there was also Constantine, and this fact as well excluded any one-sided insistence on viewing the political in demonic terms. It was certainly true that political power had been given over to the minions of the demons in order to demonstrate its low value, but it was God who had given it over, and he had from time to time also given it to those who belonged to him in order to show that he was Lord and that he did as he wished. The political and military good fortune of a Constantine and of a Theodosius indicated that one did not have to flee to the demons in order to acquire such gifts. The political was not necessarily demonic, and it did not necessarily draw its life from lying and from a disdain for justice; it could also flourish in the soil of truth and righteousness.[29] But a Christian would not call the Christian emperors happy because of their political success.

---

[28] Ibid. (Babcock, *Augustine* I, 172).
[29] See ibid., V, 24–26.

Rather, we call them happy if they rule justly; if they do
not swell with pride among the voices of those who honor
them too highly and the obsequiousness of those who
acclaim them too humbly, but remember that they are
only human beings; if they make their power the servant
of God's majesty, using it to spread the worship of God as
much as possible; if they fear, love, and worship God; if,
more than their own kingdom, they love the one where
they do not fear to have co-rulers; if they are slow to pun-
ish and quick to pardon; if they enforce punishment only
as necessary for governing and defending the republic, not
to satisfy their personal animosities; if they grant pardon
not to let wrongdoing go unpunished but in the hope
of its being corrected; if they compensate for the harsh
decisions that they are often compelled to make with the
leniency of mercy and the generosity of beneficence; if
the more they are in a position to give free rein to self-
indulgence the more they hold it in check; if they prefer
to govern their own base desires more than to govern any
peoples; if they do all this not out of a craving for empty
glory but rather out of love for eternal happiness; and if,
for their sins, they do not neglect to offer their true God
the sacrifice of humility and compassion and prayer.[30]

In this Christian "mirror of princes" there appears—for
us in a way that is particularly moving—the admonition
that the emperor, even as emperor, is supposed to remain
a human being. Political or national greatness and power
became in Augustine's portrayal a kind of mask, behind
which in the end there stood only a human being. That was

---

[30] Ibid., V, 24 (Babcock, *Augustine* I, 178, alt.). On Augustine's notion of
sacrifice, as it appears at the end of this passage, see J. Lecuyer, "Le sacrifice selon saint Augustin", in *Augustinus Magister* II (Paris, 1954), 905–14;
J. Ratzinger, "Originalität und Überlieferung in Augustins Begriff der *confes-
sio*", *Revue des Études Augustiniennes* 3 (1957): 375–92, esp. 389–92.

especially clear when he cried out to Rome, the world's proud mistress, "Cease your boasting! What are all men, after all, but men?"[31] The devaluation of national greatness opened the way to see what was common to humanity. Human-beingness was not, as it could appear at first, merely the shabby residue that was concealed behind the glittering façades of earthly power; it was in fact a positive reality that deserved to be brought forth from behind these façades. That could be seen when *humanitas* and *gratia*, humanity and grace, were mentioned in the same breath, and the person who acted in a human way appeared as someone who acted with simple and indubitable greatness.[32] It was *gratissime et humanissime*, "most graciously and humanely", that one day—much too late!—the Roman Empire made all its inhabitants citizens of Rome and thus recognized that common human identity far outweighed a previous concern with boundaries established by force of arms.[33]

4. THE PLACE OF THE CHURCH IN HISTORY

The actual driving force for the devaluation of the political, however, lay (in contrast to Stoic cosmopolitanism) not in the emphasis on the unity of human beings; that was, rather, merely the consequence of the spiritual and intellectual movement that shaped the whole of Augustine's thought—namely, the discovery of "the fatherland

[31] *City of God* V, 17.
[32] See ibid., V, 26: "He took Valentinian under his wing, preserved his imperial dignity, and consoled him with *humanity and grace*" (Babcock, *Augustine* I, 179, alt.). Ibid., V, 17: "And this would have been especially true if the Romans had immediately taken the *most gracious and humane* action that they took later on, when they granted civic standing to all who belonged to the Roman Empire so that they would be Roman citizens" (Babcock, *Augustine* I, 166).
[33] See ibid., V, 17.

on high".[34] For Augustine, earthly states and earthly father-
lands held second place, since he had found God's state,
and in it was the one fatherland of all men. No one should
succumb to any illusion here: all the states on earth were
"earthly states", even when they were ruled by Christian
emperors and inhabited more or less only by Christian
citizens. Since they were states on this earth, they were
"earthly states", and they could not be anything else.[35] As

[34] See ibid., V, 16: The expansion of the Roman Empire "also happened for
the citizens of that eternal city while they are on pilgrimage here below. It happened so that they might carefully and soberly contemplate the Roman examples, and might see how great a love they owe to their supernal *fatherland* for
the sake of eternal life, if the earthly city was so greatly loved by its citizens
for the sake of mere human glory" (Babcock, *Augustine* I, 166, alt.). Ibid., V,
17: "The city in which it is promised that we shall reign is as far removed from
this one as heaven is from earth.... The citizens of such a marvelous *fatherland*
should not think that they have done anything remarkable if, for the sake of
attaining it, they performed some good work.... And this point is especially
noteworthy because the remission of sins, which gathers citizens for the eternal
fatherland, has a kind of likeness, a sort of shadow, in the asylum established
by Romulus, where impunity for every sort of crime brought together the
multitude that was to found the city of Rome" (Babcock, *Augustine* I, 167,
alt.). Ibid., V, 18: "Is it any great thing, then, to despise all the enticements of
this world, no matter how alluring they may be, for the sake of the eternal and
heavenly *fatherland*, when, for the sake of his temporal and earthly country,
Brutus was even able to kill his own sons?" (Babcock, *Augustine* I, 167, alt.).
Ibid.: "If Regulus could do this [i.e., allow himself to be tortured for the sake of
Rome], are there any tortures that should not be despised for the sake of keeping faith with *the fatherland* to whose blessedness faith itself leads?" (Babcock,
Augustine I, 169, alt.). Examples of the Christian appropriation of the pagan
concept of *patria*, "fatherland" or "homeland", would be easy to multiply.

[35] That the *civitas terrena* or *regnum terrenum*, the "earthly city/state" or the
"earthly kingdom", refers simply to the states of this earth and to their history, including those inhabited and ruled by Christians, can be shown from
numerous texts. One need only mention ibid., V, 19 (Augustine had previously
mentioned that true virtue could only exist in tandem with the true worship
of God, and he now wanted to say that persons who, like the ancient Romans,
possessed a merely political and hence relative virtue were more useful to the
state than those who did not possess even as much as that): "Those who are
not citizens of the eternal city (which is called the city of God in our Sacred

such, they were the inevitable products of this world-age, and it was right to care for their well-being. Augustine himself loved the Roman state as his fatherland, and he was lovingly concerned with its existence.[36] But, inasmuch as all such structures once were and still continued to be earthly states, they had only a relative value and were not worthy of ultimate concern. Ultimate concern had to do only with the eternal homeland of all human beings, the *civitas caelestis*, the "heavenly city".

Here, too, we find Augustine in agreement with Origen and with the entire Christian tradition, when he is convinced that *civitas caelestis* is an apt name not only for the coming heavenly Jerusalem but also and even now for the People of God on their pilgrimage through the desert of the earthly age—in other words, for the Church.[37] In

---

Scriptures) are more useful to the earthly city when they at least have the kind of virtue that serves human glory than when they do not" (Babcock, *Augustine* I, 172–73). See also, *inter alia*, ibid., V, l; V, 12; V, 14; V, 19; V, 25; VI, 1. There are extensive citations in F. E. Cranz, "'De civitate Dei' XV, 2 et l'idée augustinienne de la société chrétienne", *Revue des Études Augustiniennes* 3 (1957): 15–27; Ratzinger, *Volk und Haus Gottes in Augustins Lehre von der Kirche*, 281–95, esp. n. 82.

[36] Particularly indicative in this regard is the kind of spontaneous remark, for example, that one can find in *City of God* IV, 7, in this case with respect to the recent sack of Rome: "The Roman Empire ... is simply afflicted, not changed into something else. The same thing has happened to it in other eras, before Christ's name was proclaimed, and it has recovered from such affliction. There is no need, then, to despair of recovery now" (Babcock, *Augustine* I, 115). For an extensive treatment of this issue, see J. Straub, "Augustinus Sorge um die Regeneratio Imperii: Das Imperium Romanum als Civitas terrena", *Historisches Jahrbuch* 73 (1954): 34–60; and also *Bibliothèque Augustinienne* 33:791–92. F. G. Maier, *Augustin und das antike Rom* (Stuttgart, 1955), is insistent on the anti-Roman thrust of Augustine's writings.

[37] On this much-discussed question, see the comprehensive and very clear proofs indicated in Cranz, "'De civitate Dei' XV, 2'", 22ff. From the numerous texts, a few examples can be cited: *City of God* XIII, 16: "But the philosophers against whose slanders we are defending the city of God—that is, his Church" (Babcock, *Augustine* II, 80). Ibid., XVI, 2: "Christ and his Church,

her is assembled from all times and peoples, from beyond the borders of the Roman Empire, the community of those who, together with God's holy angels, will form a single eternal *polis*.[38] On this earth, of course, she lives as an alien, and she can never live in any other way, because her true place is elsewhere.

So it was that the states of the world would remain earthly states until the end of the ages and that the Church would remain an alien community—likewise until the end of the ages. This was evident in the fact that the Church, in keeping with her essence, was a Church of martyrs. Augustine's theology of martyrdom was an essential part of his theology of the Church, the entity that stood over against the state, which took its life from demons. This becomes clear when he explains that the martyr is the Christian opposite of the pagan Heros. According to mythology, Heros was the son of Hera, the Greek goddess whose Roman equivalent was Juno. She was the mythological personification of what we would now call inner space ([that is, the atmosphere] in contrast to outer space), which was viewed as the abode of the demons. Demons, then, were beings that dwelled in the air; they constituted an anonymous power associated with a particular spiritual climate in accordance with which a person would direct his life and by which

---

which is the city of God" (Babcock, *Augustine* II, 187). Ibid., VIII, 24: "A house is now being built for the Lord in all the earth—namely, the city of God, which is the holy Church" (Babcock, *Augustine* I, 272). From the perspective of what these texts demonstrate, there is nothing more amazing than the ongoing denial of the equivalence of the Church and the city of God in the literature that has been influenced by idealistic thought.

[38] On Augustine's universalism, which ignores the boundaries imposed by the Roman Empire, see Peterson, "Der Monotheismus als politisches Problem", 146–47n5. On his temporal universalism, see Y. Congar, "Ecclesia ab Abel", in M. Reding, ed., *Abhandlungen über Theologie und Kirche: Festschrift Karl Adam* (Düsseldorf, 1952), 79–108.

he would let himself be ruled.[39] Heros, who belonged to
Hera and who was raised into the air, was a man who
was no longer merely a man. It was he who determined
the spiritual climate, the "air", in which one breathed
and lived. He was no longer merely a man but had obtained power, was raised up to the "principalities and powers" (Col 2:15) by which men have allowed themselves to
be led, and became a demon.[40] The Christian martyr, on
the other hand, was one who did not act in accordance
with these powers, as was customary, but who, rather,
defeated them thanks to his faith in God's greater power.
His victory consisted in suffering and in saying no to the
powers that governed the majority of people.[41] Augustine

[39] See *City of God* X, 21. I have attempted to reproduce the sense of the
Augustinian (and generally patristic) assertion that the air was the abode of
the demons in such a way as to be comprehensible to modern thinking. On
this, see Schlier, *Mächte und Gewalten im Neuen Testament*, 28ff. Of course this
existential sense was not always understood primarily in a cosmological way.
But Schlier has shown that the New Testament knew it, and that Augustine recognized it is evident throughout his discussion of the problem of the
demonic in *City of God* I–X.

[40] See *City of God* X, 21: "This term is said to be derived from Juno, since
Juno is called Hera in Greek; and therefore, according to Greek myth, one of
her sons was named Heros. In some mystic fashion, this myth supposedly signifies that the air is reckoned as Juno's province, and that is where people say
heroes dwell, along with the demons. By 'heroes' they mean the souls of the
dead marked by some special merit" (Babcock, *Augustine* I, 328–29).

[41] See ibid. for the continuation of the text from the previous note: "In
contrast, our martyrs would be called heroes (if, as I said, ecclesiastical usage
allowed) not because they are joined in community with the demons in
the air but because they defeated those very same demons—that is, those powers of the air—including Juno herself, no matter what she is supposed to signify" (Babcock, *Augustine* I, 329). Augustine then points to the fact that the
pagans try to pacify bad demons through gifts, and he continues, ibid.: "This
is not the way of true and holy religion. This is not how our martyrs defeat
Juno, that is, the powers of the air. Our heroes (if usage allowed us to call
them that) do not overcome Hera with suppliant gifts but with divine virtues"
(Babcock, *Augustine* I, 329).

saw in martyrdom the particular aspect of Christian victory in this world-age, and in the martyr he saw the sign of the Church, which lived and conquered in this world under the form of suffering.

The bishop of Hippo thus came to terms not only with the reality of and even the necessity for the state but also with its imperfection—or, more correctly, with the imperfection of all the states—in this world. To that extent, the eschatological radicalness of the Christian revolution is considerably more measured in him than it is in Origen. The difference in their positions is also evident in their conception of the unification of mankind. Both Origen and Augustine followed the late Jewish and early Christian tradition of seeing the division of mankind into nations primarily from the perspective of the problem of language: men were unavoidably cut off from one another by the vast number of different languages.[42] Both Origen and Augustine saw in this confusion of languages the sign of the sinfulness that was to be conquered in Christ Jesus. For his part, Origen's gaze went immediately to the *eschaton*, when everyone would speak a single language; at that point, the unity of mankind would be reestablished. The unity of language was an exclusively eschatological gift; only at the *eschaton* would the hope for it be fulfilled.[43]

Augustine viewed the issue differently. He very emphatically set the miracle of the tongues at Pentecost (Acts 2:1–13) over against the Babylonian confusion of languages. But, while for Origen the miracle of Pentecost remained a onetime eschatological sign, Augustine saw in it a kind

---

[42] For proofs of this, see Peterson, "Das Problem des Nationalismus im alten Christentum", 61–62, and n. 35.

[43] See ibid., 62n35. On the mystical-spiritualizing interpretation that Origen gives along with the eschatological, see n. 47.

of symbol of what was happening in the Church on an ongoing basis—namely, that the one Church encompassed all lands and languages and that the community of love for the Lord embraced those who were linguistically separated from one another. In the body of Christ, where all languages were spoken, the miracle of Pentecost was an enduring phenomenon. In Augustine's words:

> Why are you unwilling to speak in the languages of all? Every tongue resounded there. How is it that today a person to whom the Holy Spirit has been given does not speak in the tongues of all? At that date it was a sign that the Holy Spirit had come upon people when they spoke in all languages. What are you going to say now, you heretic? That the Holy Spirit is not given? . . . But if he is given, why do those to whom he is given not speak in the tongues of all peoples? . . . Why then does the Holy Spirit not manifest himself today in the multiplicity of languages? But he does; he is manifest today in all tongues. At the beginning the Church was not spread throughout the entire world, making it possible for Christ's members to speak among all nations, and therefore the miracle happened in each person as a presage of what would later be true of all. Today the whole body of Christ does speak in the languages of all peoples, or, rather, if there are any tongues in which it does not yet speak, it will. The Church will grow until it claims all languages as its own. . . . I dare to say to you, "I speak in the tongues of all. I am in Christ's body, I am in Christ's Church. If Christ's body today speaks in the languages of all, I too speak in all languages. Greek is mine, Syriac is mine, Hebrew is mine. Mine is the tongue of every nation, because I am within the unity that embraces all nations."[44]

[44] *Exposition of Psalm 147*, 19, trans. M. Boulding, *The Works of Saint Augustine* III, 20 (Hyde Park, N.Y., 2004), 464, alt.

What that tower [of Babel] had disunited the Church is bringing together. Many tongues were made out of one; do not be surprised, pride did this. One tongue is being made out of many; do not be surprised, charity did this.[45]

For Augustine, becoming a Christian essentially meant going from a scattered existence to unity, from the Tower of Babel to the upper room of Pentecost, from the many peoples of the human race to one new people.[46]

It would be an attractive project, but one too ambitious for the present essay, to compare these two theologies of language—Origen's eschatological theology (which is joined in his writings to a time-transcending mystical, spiritualizing theology)[47] and Augustine's ecclesiastical-sacramental

---

[45] *Homily on the Gospel of John* 6,10, trans. E. Hill, *The Works of Saint Augustine* III, 12 (Hyde Park, N.Y., 2009), 130.

[46] See Ratzinger, *Volk und Haus Gottes in Augustins Lehre von der Kirche*, 127–58, esp. n. 82, which indicates with numerous references how, in his debate with the Donatists, Augustine was increasingly drawn to see the core of Christian existence in that concrete *caritas* by way of which *omnes gentes* would be brought together into *una gens*. One text may suffice for the many that could be adduced. See *Answer to the Letters of Petilian* III, 3, 4: "And when they [i.e., the Donatists] flee from communion with those men [i.e., immoral Catholics], as persons whom they know, they are abandoning unity with it [i.e., the Church], when, if the charity that endures all things were in them (1 Cor 13:7), they would instead put up with what they know in one nation (*una gente*), lest they cut themselves off from the good to whom, among all the nations (*omnibus gentibus*), they were unable to teach alien and bad things."

[47] See *Against Celsus* VIII, 22: The Christian "is always living in the days of Pentecost, and particularly when, like the apostles of Jesus, he goes up to the upper room and gives time to supplication and prayer, so that he becomes worthy of the mighty rushing wind from heaven which compels the evil in men and its consequences to disappear, and so that he becomes worthy also of some share in the fiery tongue given by God" (Chadwick, *Origen*, 468). See also Origen, *Homily on Jeremiah* 20, 1–7. This style of interpretation lies on a purely individual and interior level, whereas, in *Against Celsus* V, 29–31, the visibly developing hope in a unified language is purely eschatological. The eschatological concept of a unification of language is clearer in Filastrius of Brescia, *A*

theology[48]—with the third one that was developed along
the political-theocratic lines set down by Eusebius of Cae-
sarea, according to which the eschatological unification of
languages was accomplished in the unity of the imperial
language of New Rome.[49] Eusebius' theology is significant
in that it equated Christian universalism with Rome's universal empire; in so doing, it dragged down that universalism to a political level and thus robbed it of its breadth
and depth. The door had now been opened to nationalism,
which was once again able to fix itself on an actual political
entity.[50] In Augustine, in contrast, the newness that Christianity introduced was evident. His doctrine of two states, or
cities, aimed neither at a state dominated by the Church nor
at a Church dominated by the state. Its goal, rather, was—in
the midst of the structures of this world, which remained
and indeed had to remain what they were—to offer the
new power of faith in the unity of men within the body
of Christ as an element of a transformation whose ultimate
form would be shaped by God himself, when history had
finally completed its course.

Book of the Various Heresies, 76–77. Augustine's ecclesiastical interpretation thus
stands in the middle between a purely mystical and spiritualizing approach, on
the one hand, and a purely eschatological approach, on the other.

[48] One may speak of a sacramental understanding inasmuch as, for Augustine, *caritas* is closely connected to *communio*. See Ratzinger, *Volk und Haus
Gottes in Augustins Lehre von der Kirche*, 136–58, esp. n. 82.

[49] See the texts cited in Peterson, "Das Problem des Nationalismus im alten
Christentum", 62n35. Peterson refers to O. Treitinger, *Die oströmische Kaiser-
und Reichsidee* (Jena, 1958), 165.

[50] On the imperial theology of Eusebius, see Peterson, "Der Monotheismus als politisches Problem", 86–93n5; Cranz, "'De civitate Dei' XV, 2",
24–27n107, which lists further literature. A well thought-out and more positive
view of the theology that originated with Eusebius is offered in E. von Ivanka,
Rhomäerreich und Gottesvolk (Freiburg, 1968). Ivanka emphasizes the Old Testament components of the Byzantine idea of empire, which in no way can
be understood simply as a Christian development of the pagan concept of the
empire ruled by a divine emperor.

5. CONCLUSION

In conclusion, it is important to note that Augustine himself did not attempt to work out what a world that had
embraced Christianity would look like. His city of God, to
be sure, is not a purely ideal community composed entirely
of all the people who believe in God, but neither does
it have anything to do with an earthly theocracy, with a
world that is established along Christian lines; it is, rather, a
sacramental-eschatological entity, which lives in this world
as a sign of the coming world.[51] The fragility inherent in
the idea of a Christian world was made clear to Augustine in the year 410, when it was not merely the pagans
who clamored for Rome's ancient gods.[52] Hence, the state
remained for him, in all its real or apparent Christianiza-
tion, an earthly state, and the Church remained an alien
community that accepted and used the earthly but was not
at home in it. To be sure, the coexistence of the two communities was more peaceful in Augustine's time than it

[51] For this whole concept and its limitations in comparison with other
interpretations, apart from what has already been discussed, see J. Ratzinger,
"Herkunft und Sinn der Civitas-Lehre Augustins", in Congrès International
Augustinien, *Augustinus Magister* II (Paris, 1954), 965–79. Although I sought
to distinguish my "sacramental" interpretation from the purely eschatological
interpretation of W. Kamlah, it is still obvious that, in Augustine's view, the
sacramental and the eschatological are complementary. As a *communio caritatis*,
the Church remains an alien in this world; she is neither an earthly state nor
a theocracy but rather achieves her end at the *eschaton*. To that extent, Augustine's sacramental view of the Church maintains rather than does away with an
eschatological perspective. That my own interpretation of *The City of God* has
been completely misunderstood by U. Duchrow in his *Christenheit und Welt-
verantwortung* (Stuttgart, 1970), 235–36, should be quite clear from the explanations in the book, which he did not take into consideration (despite the fact that
it was available to him). Likewise, A. Wachtel's similar lack of understanding in
his *Beiträge zur Geschichtstheologie des Aurelius Augustinus* (Bonn, 1960) could be
corrected by considering those explanations.

[52] On the position of paganism in the Roman Empire during Augustine's
time, see *Bibliothèque Augustinienne* 33:175–83.

was in Origen's. Augustine never spoke of plotting against the "Scythian" state; rather, he felt that it was justifiable for Christians, who were members of the eternal home-land, to serve in Babylon as officials and even as emperors. Thus, while in Origen one does not see how this world is supposed to keep going but must simply be ready for the breakthrough of the *eschaton*, Augustine not only counted on the Roman Empire's continuation but even consid-ered the empire so central to the world-age in which he lived that he wished for its renewal. He remained true to eschatological thinking, however, insofar as he viewed the whole world as provisional and, consequently, did not attempt to give it a Christian constitution; instead, he let it remain as it was and allowed it to struggle with its own relative structure. To that extent, the Christianity that was now lawful by intention was also revolutionary in an ulti-mate sense, since it could not be identified with any state but was, rather, a force that relativized everything that was included in the world by pointing to the one absolute God and to the one Mediator between God and man, Jesus Christ (1 Tim 2:5).[53]

---

[53] For this reason, it is completely erroneous to use the *compelle intrare* of the Donatist struggle to make Augustine the father of the theocratic ecclesiastical constitution of the Middle Ages, even when so-called medieval Augustinianism appealed to him in that regard. The imperial assistance that Augustine hesitat-ingly accepted against the Donatist partisans known as Circumcellions, and ultimately against the Donatist movement as a whole, neither did away with his basic position regarding the "earthly city" nor, considering the situation, really contradicted it. One cannot rightly make Augustine himself responsi-ble for the false interpretation that was later attached to the Catholic response to Donatism. On the political Augustinianism of the Middle Ages, see H. X. Arquillière, *L'augustinisme politique: Essai sur la formation des théories politiques au moyen âge* (Paris, 1956); Arquillière, "Réflexions sur l'essence de l'augustinisme politique", in *Augustinus Magister* 2:991–1002. On Augustine's understanding of the political, see the extensive bibliography in *Bibliothèque Augustinienne* 33:156–59.

V

Christians Faced with Forms of Totalitarianism

Homily in Bonn
(November 26, 1981)

The reading and the Gospel that we have just heard stemmed from a situation in which Christians were not a self-organizing subject of the state but were, rather, outcasts being persecuted by a cruel dictatorship. They themselves were not allowed to share the responsibility for their state; they could only endure it. Theirs was not the privilege of shaping it as a Christian state but was rather the task of living as Christians in spite of it. The names of the

This homily was given on November 26, 1981, during a liturgy for Catholic representatives to the *Bundestag* [the Lower House of the German Federal Republic] in the Church of Saint Winfried [Saint Boniface] in Bonn. The readings, 1 Peter 1:3–7 and John 14:1–6, were prescribed by the Church's liturgy for that day. At first they seemed unsuited to the subject, but, on second thought, after closer inspection, they proved to be unexpectedly rich material for this meditation.

From Joseph Ratzinger / Pope Benedict XVI, "Biblical Aspects of the Theme of Faith and Politics", in *Church, Ecumenism, and Politics: New Endeavors in Ecclesiology*, trans. Michael J. Miller et al. (San Francisco: Ignatius Press, 2008), 143–47.

emperors who reigned during the period to which tradition dates both texts are enough to make the situation clear: Nero and Domitian. And so the First Letter of Peter, too, calls the Christians in such a state strangers or "exiles" (1:1) and the state itself "Babylon" (5:13). In doing so, it very emphatically indicates the political position of the Christians of that time, which corresponded roughly to the position of the exiled Jews living in Babylon, who were not the subjects but, rather, the objects of that state and therefore had to learn how they could survive in it, since they were not allowed to learn how to build it. Thus, the political background of today's readings is fundamentally different from ours. Nevertheless, they contain three important statements that have significance also for political action among Christians.

1. The state is not the whole of human existence and does not encompass all human hope. Man and what he hopes for extend beyond the framework of the state and beyond the sphere of political action. This is true not only for a state like Babylon, but for every state. The state is not the totality; this unburdens the politician and at the same time opens up for him the path of reasonable politics. The Roman state was wrong and anti-Christian precisely because it wanted to be the totality of human possibilities and hopes. A state that makes such claims cannot fulfill its promises; it thereby falsifies and diminishes man. Through the totalitarian lie, it becomes demonic and tyrannical. The abolition of the totalitarian state has demythologized the state and thereby liberated man as well as politicians and politics.

But when the Christian faith falls into ruins and faith in mankind's greater hope is lost, the myth of the divine state rises again, because man cannot do without the totality of hope. Although such promises pose as progress and commandeer for themselves the slogans of progress and progressive thinking, viewed historically they are nevertheless a regression to an era antedating the *novum* of Christianity, a turning back along the scale of history. And even though their propaganda says that their goal is man's complete liberation, the abolition of all ruling authority, they contradict the truth of man and are opposed to his freedom, because they force man to fit into what he himself can make. Such politics, which declares that the kingdom of God is the outcome of politics and twists faith into the universal primacy of the political, is by its very nature the politics of enslavement; it is mythological politics.

To this, faith opposes Christian reason's sense of proportion, which recognizes what man really can accomplish in terms of a free social order and is content with that, because it knows that mankind's greater expectations are safe in God's hands. To renounce the hope of faith is at the same time to renounce political reason and its sense of proportion. Abandoning the mythical hopes of an authority-free society is not resignation but honesty, which sustains man in hope. The mythical hope of a self-made paradise can only drive man into inescapable anxiety—into fear of the failure of the illusory promises and of the immense emptiness that lurks behind them; into fear of his own power and of its cruelty.

Thus the first service to politics rendered by the Christian faith is that it liberates man from the irrationality of political myths, which are the real threat of our time. Taking a stand for sobriety, which does what is possible and does not cry with an ardent heart after the impossible, is of course always difficult; the voice of reason is not as loud as the cry of unreason.

The cry for the grandiose project has the cachet of morality; restricting oneself to what is possible, in contrast, seems to be the renunciation of moral passion, mere fainthearted pragmatism. But, as a matter of fact, political morality consists precisely of resisting the seductive force of the big words for which humanity and its chances are being gambled away. The moral thing is not adventurous moralism, which tries to mind God's business, but rather honesty, which accepts man's limits and does man's work within them. Not the uncompromising stance, but compromise is the true morality in political matters.

2. Although the Christians were being persecuted, they did not have a negative view of the state in principle, but, rather, they still recognized in it the state *qua* state and did what was in their power to build it up as a state; they did not try to destroy it. Precisely because they knew that they were in "Babylon", they applied to themselves the guidelines that Jeremiah had written to the children of Israel who had been exiled to that place. The letter of the prophet that is recorded in chapter 29 of the Book of Jeremiah was by no means an activist's manual calling for political resistance and the destruction of the slave state, as understandable as that would have been; it is, rather, an instruction on how to preserve and strengthen what is good. Thus, it is a lesson in surviving and at the same time in preparing for better days and new prospects. In that sense, this morality of exile also contains basic elements of a positive political ethos. Jeremiah urges the Jews not to persist in contradiction and denial but, rather, to "build houses and live in them; plant gardens and eat their produce.... Seek the welfare of the city where I have sent you into exile, and pray to the LORD on its behalf, for in its welfare you will find your welfare" (Jer 29:5–7). We can read a very similar admonition in

Paul's First Letter to Timothy, which tradition dates to
the time of Nero, where it says to pray "for all men, for
kings and all who are in high positions, that we may lead a
quiet and peaceable life, godly and respectful in every way"
(1 Tim 2:1–2). Along the same lines, the First Letter of
Peter itself admonishes the readers to "maintain good conduct among the Gentiles, so that in case they speak against
you as wrongdoers, they may see your good deeds and glorify God on the day of visitation" (2:12). "Honor all men.
Love the brotherhood. Fear God. Honor the emperor"
(2:17). "But let none of you suffer as a murderer, or a thief,
or a wrongdoer, or a mischief-maker; yet if one suffers as
a Christian, let him not be ashamed, but under that name
let him glorify God" (4:15f.).

What does this mean? The Christians were by no
means fearful, gullible people who were taken in by the
authorities and did not know that there can be a right to
resistance and even a conscientious duty to resist. The
very last sentence shows that they recognized the limits of the state and did not bow to it in matters where
they were not allowed to bow to it because it opposed
God's will. Even more importantly, the fact remains that
they still did not attempt to destroy that state; rather, they
tried to build it up. Amorality is fought by morality, and
evil by a determined adherence to the good, and in no
other way. Morality—doing good—is the true resistance,
and only the good can be a preparation for a turn for the
better. There are not two kinds of political morality: a
morality of resistance and a morality of ruling. There is
only one morality: morality as such, the morality of God's
commandments, which cannot be temporarily suspended
in order to bring about a change in the status quo more
quickly. One can build up only by building up, not by
destroying—that is the political ethics of the Bible from

Jeremiah to Peter and Paul. The Christian always supports the state, in *this* sense: he does the positive, the good things that hold states together. He has no fear that he will thereby favor the power of the wicked, but he is convinced that evil can be dismantled and the power of evil and of evil men can be diminished only by strengthening what is good. Anyone who accepts the killing of the innocent and the destruction of other people's property as part of the bargain cannot appeal to the faith. The words of Saint Peter are quite explicitly against such methods: "Let none of you suffer [condemnation] as a murderer, or a thief" (4:15)—and at that time he was speaking also against this sort of resistance. The true, Christian resistance that he is demanding occurs only in the situation where the state demands the repudiation of God and of his commandments, where it demands evil, against which good is still commanded.

3. A final point follows logically from this. The Christian faith destroyed the myth of the divine state, the myth of the earthly paradise or utopian state and of a society without rule. In its place, it put the objectivity of reason. But that does not mean that it brought an objectivity devoid of values, the objectivity of statistics and mere social dynamics. True human objectivity involves humanity, and humanity involves God. True human reason involves morality, which lives on God's commandments. This morality is not a private matter; it has public significance. Without the good of being good and of good action, there can be no good politics. What the persecuted Church prescribed for Christians as the core of their political ethos must also be the core of an active Christian politics: only where good is done and is recognized as good can people live together well in a thriving community. Demonstrating the practical

importance of the moral dimension, the dimension of God's commandments—publicly as well—must be the center of responsible political action.

If we act in this way, then even in the midst of confusion and adversity we can understand the words from today's Scriptures as a reliable promise addressed to us personally: "Let not your hearts be troubled" (Jn 14:1). "By God's power [you] are guarded through faith for a salvation ready to be revealed" (1 Pet 1:5). Amen.

VI

Truth, Values, Power

Touchstones of Pluralistic Society

FOREWORD

The three essays that are collected in this little volume originated on altogether different occasions, although in each case as a result of the same underlying question. The first essay is the German version of the speech in November 1992 in the ceremonial hall of the Académie Française to express my gratitude for being inducted into the section for Moral and Political Sciences. In keeping with tradition, the new member has to offer an appreciation of his predecessor, whose vacated seat he now takes. In my case, it was Andrei Sakharov, and thus the topic was set, too. Sakharov was great as a physicist, but he was above all great as a human being, as a passionate and fearless fighter for human dignity and freedom. He accepted the price of suffering imposed on him by the Communist regime,

Wahrheit, Werte, Macht: Prüfsteine einer pluralistischen Gesellschaft, 2nd ed. (1993; Freiburg im Breisgau: Herder, 1994). Section (a) translated by Michael J. Miller; section (b) previously published in *On Conscience* (Philadelphia: National Catholic Bioethics Center; San Francisco: Ignatius Press, 2007), 11–41; section (c) was previously published as chapter 4 of *Values in a Time of Upheaval: Meeting the Challenges of the Future*, trans. Brian McNeil (San Francisco: 2014), 53–72.

whose mendacity and inhumanity he unmasked before the
eyes of the world public. This public admired him, but at
the same time it was unwilling to stop flirting with the ideology on account of which he suffered. According to the
traditions of the Academy, my speech could not just be an
obituary, a merely retrospective appreciation of my great
predecessor; his figure raised the question of how today
and in principle a national community should be shaped in
freedom: it was necessary to reflect on the ethical content
of human freedom as a reality that always can be lived only
in shared responsibility.

The time frame provided allowed room only for rather
aphoristic indications of several rather important aspects.
In this attempt, I was able to refer to a speech that I had
given in the spring of 1992 in the Slovak capital Bratislava
before a large audience. After the end of the Communist
dictatorship, the question arose there with great urgency
and quite concretely of how a new and just state is to
be built, how freedom can be preserved and shaped as
freedom in justice. The Paris lecture and the speech in
Bratislava, which is reprinted in this book as the third
essay, therefore mesh very closely; in Paris, I only tried
to elucidate once more, in terms of the concrete figure
of Sakharov, statements on the subject that I had already
presented in the capital of Slovakia.

The second essay in this little volume was first drafted
for the workshop of American bishops in Dallas in the
spring of 1991, where questions about the foundation
of moral theology were to be debated. In its German
version, it was dedicated to my colleague and friend
in Tübingen, Max Seckler, on the occasion of his sixty-
fifth birthday; it was first published in the *Festschrift* [com-
memorative volume] for this occasion. The questions that
it poses are prior to those in the first and third essays and

in a certain respect can be viewed at the same time as their foundation. Only when man has internalized morality and in his innermost being reaches beyond himself are morality and freedom not antithetical but, rather, mutually dependent realities that build on one another. Thus the question about political freedom must start with the question of moral freedom, and the latter in turn must try to clarify where each individual gets his identity, his truth. At this point, the question about God undeniably enters into the question about man; the question about God, in turn, cannot be posed abstractly, since it is inseparable from the encounter of human history with Jesus Christ. This approach outlines difficult problems, and I did not want to treat them simply in a purely theoretical way; I tried to develop them from concrete experiences of my own intellectual path. My hope is that in precisely this way what is essential may be demonstrated graphically, in its human realism, beyond mere scholarly platitudes.

Rome, August 6, 1993
Joseph Cardinal Ratzinger

1. FREEDOM, LAW, AND THE GOOD: MORAL PRINCIPLES IN DEMOCRATIC SOCIETIES

It is a great honor for me to be able from now on to belong to the Institut de France by following the great figure of Andrei Dmitrievich Sakharov. I am sincerely grateful for it. Sakharov was among the important representatives of his science, physics, but he was more than an important

Speech given on the occasion of my induction as a foreign associate member into the Académie des Sciences Morales et Politiques of the Institut de France on November 7, 1992, in Paris.

scientist: he was a great man. He fought for the humanity of man, for his ethical dignity and his freedom, and therefore also accepted the price of suffering, persecution, and the renunciation of the possibility of doing further scientific work. Science can serve mankind, but it can also become an instrument of evil and then bestow on the latter its full horror. Only when it is undergirded by ethical responsibility is it capable of realizing its true essence.

a. The Public Claim of Conscience

I do not know when or how this relation of science to ethics became clear to Sakharov in all its seriousness. A short note concerning an incident from the year 1955 gives some indication. In November 1955, very important thermonuclear weapons tests had been started, which resulted in tragic events: the death of a young soldier and of a young twelve-year-old girl. During a little banquet that followed, Sakharov proposed a toast in which he expressed his hope that Russian weapons would never explode over cities. The one in charge of the test, a high-ranking officer, declared in his response that the job of scientists was to improve weapons, and the way in which they were utilized was not their business; their understanding, he thought, was not competent for that. Sakharov commented on this remark, saying that he already believed then what he still believes today: namely, "that no man whatsoever can reject his share of the responsibility for a matter on which the existence of mankind depends."[1] Basically, the officer—perhaps without realizing it—had refused to acknowledge that ethics has its own dimension in which every person is competent. In his view, apparently, only special competencies

---

[1] See Andrej Dimitrijewitsch Sacharow, *Mein Land und die Welt* (Vienna, Munich, and Zurich: Fritz Molder Verlag, 1976), 82.

of a scientific, political, and military nature exist. In truth, there is no special competency that could confer the right to kill human beings or to have them killed. The denial of the general human capacity to judge what concerns man as man creates a new class system and thereby degrades everyone, because then man no longer exists as such. The negation of the ethical principle, the negation of this organ of knowledge, prior to any specialization, which we call conscience, is the negation of man. Again and again, Sakharov pointed out with great insistence this responsibility of each individual for the whole and found his own mission in safeguarding this responsibility.

As of 1968, he was excluded from projects involving state secrets; he advocated all the more the public rights of conscience. His thought gravitated from then on around human rights, around the moral renewal of the country and of mankind, and, in general, around universal human values and the dictates of conscience. He who loved his country so much had to become the accuser of a regime that drove men to apathy, lethargy, and indifference, which reduced them to exterior and interior poverty. One could of course say that with the fall of the Communist system, Sakharov's mission was accomplished; that it was an important chapter in the history of political morality but one that now belongs to the past. I think that such an idea would be a big mistake and a dangerous one. First of all, it is clear that the general orientation of Sakharov's thought toward human dignity and human rights, obedience to the conscience, even at the price of suffering, remains a message that does not lose its relevance even when the political context no longer exists in which this message acquired its own relevance.

Moreover, I think that the threats to mankind that, with the domination of Marxist parties, had become concrete political forces that were destroying mankind persist even today under other forms.

Robert Spaemann recently said that nowadays, after the fall of utopia, a banal nihilism is beginning to spread, the consequences of which could prove to be just as dangerous.[2] He mentions as an example the American philosopher Richard Rorty, who formulated the new utopia of banality. Rorty's ideal is a liberal society in which absolute values and standards will no longer exist; the only thing worth the trouble of pursuing will be well-being. In his circumspect but altogether determined critique of the Western world, Sakharov anticipated the danger looming in this emptying out of what is human when he spoke about the "leftist-liberal fashion" or denounced the naïveté and cynicism that often paralyze the West when it comes to assuming its moral responsibility.[3]

b. Individual Freedom and Common Values

Here we are confronted with the problem that Sakharov poses to us today: How can the free world do justice to its moral responsibility? Freedom keeps its dignity only if it stays connected with its ethical foundation and mission. A freedom that consisted solely of being able to satisfy one's needs would not be a human freedom; it would remain in the animal realm. Deprived of its content, individual freedom abolishes itself, because the individual's freedom can exist only in an order of freedoms. Freedom needs a communal content that we could define as the guarantee of human rights. To put it another way: the concept of freedom by its very essence calls for supplementation by

---

[2] Robert Spaemann, "La perle précieuse et le nihilisme banal", *Catholica* 33 (1992): 43–50 at 45.

[3] Sacharow, *Mein Land*, 17; see also 44f. and passim.

two other concepts: law and the good. We could say that part of freedom is the ability of the conscience to perceive the fundamental values of mankind that concern everyone.

On this point we must continue Sakharov's thought today so as to transpose it appropriately to the present situation. Sakharov was grateful to the free world for its support of his cause and its advocacy on behalf of others who were being persecuted, and yet tragically he experienced the failure of the West again and again in many political events and with regard to the personal fates of many. He did not consider it his task to analyze the deeper motives for this, but nonetheless he saw clearly that freedom is often understood egotistically and superficially.[4] One cannot wish for freedom for oneself alone; freedom is indivisible and must always be regarded as a mission for all mankind. This means that one cannot have it without sacrifices and renunciation. It demands that we take care that morality, as a public, communal tie, is understood in such a way that, although it is powerless in itself, people acknowledge its true power at the service of mankind. Freedom demands that governments and all who have responsibility bow before what stands there defenseless by itself and cannot exercise coercion.

Here lies the threat to modern democracies with which we must grapple along the lines of Sakharov's thought. It is difficult to see how democracy, which is based on the principle of majority rule, can uphold moral values that are not supported by a majority without introducing a dogmatism that is foreign to it. On this subject, Rorty thinks that reason guided by the majority always includes several intuitive ideas, for example, the abolition of slavery. Pierre Bayle in the seventeenth century

---

[4] See, for example, ibid., 21f., 89.

expressed himself much more optimistically. At the end of
the bloody wars into which the major controversies about
faith had thrown Europe, he thought that metaphysics did
not affect political life; practical truth was sufficient. In his
view, there was only one universal and necessary morality, which was a clear, true light that all men perceive
as soon as they open their eyes.[5] Bayle's ideas reflect the
intellectual-historical situation of his century: the unity
of faith had disintegrated; one could no longer take as a
common good the truths of the metaphysical realm. But
the essential fundamental moral convictions with which
Christianity had formed souls were still unquestioned cer-
titudes, and it seemed that unaided reason could perceive
their purely evident character.

The events of this century have taught us that there is
no such evidence that can serve as a permanent, sure basis
of all freedoms. Reason can very well lose sight of the
essential values; even the intuition on which Rorty relies
has its limits. For instance, the idea that he mentions, that
slavery should be abolished, did not exist for centuries, and
the history of the totalitarian states of our century shows
clearly enough how easily it can be denied again. Freedom
can abolish itself, become disgusted with itself, once it has
become empty. We have seen that, too, in our century: a
majority decision can serve to rescind freedom.

At the root of the uneasiness that Sakharov felt when
confronted by the naïveté and cynicism of the West is this
problem of an empty, aimless freedom. When the principle of majority rule is absolutized, someday the strict positivism expressed thereby inevitably turns into nihilism. We

---

[5] See Vittorio Possenti, *Le società liberali al bivio: Lineamenti di filosofia della
società* (Genoa: Marietti, 1991), 293; see also "The Significance of Ethical and
Religious Values in a Pluralistic Society", 131–51, below.

must counteract this danger when it comes to defending freedom and human rights.

In 1938, Hermann Rauschning, a politician from Danzig, diagnosed National Socialism as a nihilist revolution: "There was and there is no goal that National Socialism would not be ready to abandon or to set at any time for the sake of the movement."[6] National Socialism was only an instrument that nihilism utilized but was also ready to get rid of at any time so as to replace it with something else. It seems to me that even the incidents that we are observing with some uneasiness in Germany today cannot be adequately explained by the label of xenophobia. At bottom here too, ultimately, there is a nihilism that comes from the emptiness of souls: in the National Socialist dictatorship as in the Communist one, there was no activity that would have been regarded as bad in itself and always immoral. Whatever served the goals of the movement or of the Party was good, however inhumane it might be. Thus, over the decades, the moral sense has been trampled on, and this necessarily becomes complete nihilism at the moment when none of the previous goals has value any longer and freedom is reduced to the possibility of doing anything that might make an empty life exciting and interesting for a moment.

c. Respecting a Core of Humanity

Let us return to the question of how to reinforce law and the good in our societies against naïveté and cynicism without imposing this force of law or defining it arbitrarily

[6] Hermann Rauschning, Die Revolution des Nihilismus (Zurich: Europa Verlag, 1938; new abridged edition by Golo Mann, Zurich: Europa Verlag, 1964). Compare Joseph Ratzinger, Church, Ecumenism, and Politics, trans. Michael J. Miller (San Francisco: Ignatius Press, 2008), 160–72.

through external coercion. In this regard, Tocqueville's analysis of *Democracy in America* always impressed me. In order for this inherently brittle structure nonetheless to hold together and to make possible an order of freedoms in communally lived freedom, this great political thinker saw as an essential prerequisite the fact that in America a fundamental moral conviction nourished by Protestant Christianity was alive, which first gave to its institutions and democratic mechanisms their supporting foundations.[7] Indeed, institutions cannot be maintained and work without common ethical convictions. These, however, cannot come from purely empirical reason. Even majority decisions will remain truly human and reasonable only insofar as they presuppose a core of humanity and respect it as the genuine common good, the prerequisite for all other goods. These convictions demand corresponding human attitudes, and these attitudes cannot flourish when the historical foundation of a culture and the ethical-religious insights that it contains are not taken into consideration. For a culture and a nation to cut themselves off from the great ethical and religious forces of their own history is for them to commit suicide. To cultivate the essential moral judgments, to preserve and to protect them as a common good without imposing them coercively seems to me to be a condition for the continuance of freedom as opposed to all sorts of nihilism and their totalitarian consequences.

I see this also as the public mission of the Christian churches in today's world. It is in keeping with the nature of the Church that she is separate from the state and that her faith cannot be imposed by the state but, rather, is

---

[7] André Jardin, *Tocqueville: A Biography*, trans. Lydia David and Robert Hemenway (New York: Macmillan, 1989), 218 and passim.

based on freely acquired convictions. On this point, there is a beautiful saying by Origen that, unfortunately, has not always been sufficiently heeded: "Christ triumphs over no one unless he himself wants it. He triumphs only by convincing: for he is the WORD of God."[8] The Church's business is not to be a state or a part of the state but, rather, to be a community based on convictions. But it is also her business to realize that she is responsible for everything and cannot limit herself to her own concerns. With the freedom that belongs to her, she must address everyone's freedom in such a way that the moral forces of history remain the forces of the present day and that there is an ongoing resurgence of the values without which common freedom is not possible.

2. IF YOU WANT TRUTH, RESPECT THE CONSCIENCE OF EVERY PERSON: CONSCIENCE AND TRUTH

In the contemporary discussion on what constitutes the essence of morality and how it can be recognized, the question of conscience has become paramount, especially in the field of Catholic moral theology. This discussion centers on the concepts of freedom and norm, autonomy and

---

[8] Origen, *Fragments on the Psalms* 4, 1: *PG* 12:1133B; cf. Maurice Geerard, *Clavis Patrum Graecorum* I (Turnhout: Brepols, 1983), 151. German translation: Hans Urs von Balthasar, *Geist und Feuer*, 3rd ed. (Einsiedeln: Johannes Verlag, 1991), 277.

"Wenn du den Frieden willst, achte das Gewissen jedes Menschen: Gewissen und Wahrheit", translated as "Conscience and Truth", in Joseph Cardinal Ratzinger, *On Conscience* (San Francisco: Ignatius Press; Philadelphia: National Catholic Bioethics Society, 2007), 11–41.

Keynote address of the Tenth Bishops' Workshop of the National Catholic Bioethics Center, on "Catholic Conscience: Foundation and Formation", February 1991.

heteronomy, self-determination and external determination by authority.

Conscience appears here as the bulwark of freedom in contrast to encroachments of authority on existence. In this, two notions of the Catholic are set in opposition to each other. One is a renewed understanding of the Catholic essence, which expounds Christian faith from the basis of freedom and as the very principle of freedom itself. The other is a superseded, "preconciliar" model, which subjects Christian existence to authority, regulating life even in its most intimate preserves, and thereby attempts to maintain control over people's lives. Morality of conscience and morality of authority, as two opposing models, appear to be locked in a struggle with each other. Accordingly, the freedom of the Christian would be rescued by appeal to the classical principle of moral tradition: that conscience is the highest norm that man is to follow, even in opposition to authority. Authority—in this case, the Magisterium—may well speak of matters moral, but only in the sense of presenting conscience with material for its own deliberation. Conscience would retain, however, the final word. Some authors reduce conscience in this, its aspect of final arbiter, to the formula "conscience is infallible."[9]

---

[9] This thesis was apparently first proposed by J. G. Fichte: "Conscience does [not] and cannot err", because it is "itself judge of all conviction", which "recognizes no higher judge over itself. It is the ultimate authority and cannot be appealed" (*System der Sittenlehre* [1798], III, 15; reprinted in *Fichtes Werke*, vol. 4, ed. I. M. Fichte [Berlin: de Gruyter, 1971], 174). See H. Reiner, "Gewissen", in J. Ritter and K. Grunder, eds.: *Historisches Wörterbuch der Philosophie* 3 (1974): 574–92, here 586. Kant had already previously formulated the counterarguments. They appear in more depth in Hegel, for whom conscience "as formal subjectivity ... [is] always on the verge of changing into evil" (see Reiner, "Gewissen"). Nevertheless, the thesis of the infallibility of conscience is at present again in the ascendancy in popular theological literature. I find a—in a certain respect—mediating position in E. Schockenhoff, *Das umstrittene Gewissen* (Mainz, Germany: 1990), which expressly reckons with the possibility that conscience can miss its mark "by going astray of the other requirement of

Nonetheless, at this point a contradiction can arise. It is, of course, undisputed that one must follow a certain conscience, or at least not act against it. But whether the judgment of conscience, or what one takes to be such, is always right—indeed, whether it is infallible—is another question. For if this were the case, it would mean that there is no truth—at least not in moral and religious matters, which is to say, in the areas that constitute the very pillars of our existence. For judgments of conscience can contradict each other. Thus there could be, at best, the subject's own truth, which would be reduced to the subject's sincerity. No door or window would lead from the subject into the broader world of being and human solidarity. Whoever thinks this through will come to the realization that no real freedom exists, then, and that the supposed pronouncements of conscience are but the reflection of social circumstances. This should necessarily lead to the conclusion that placing freedom in opposition to authority overlooks something. There must be something deeper if freedom and, therefore, human existence are to have meaning.

a. A Conversation on the Erroneous Conscience and First Inferences

It has become apparent that the question of conscience leads in fact to the core of the moral problem and, thus, to the question of man's existence itself. I would now

---

the moral law, the mutual recognition of the free rational being" (139). Schockenhoff, however—relying on [F. X.] Linsenmann—rejects talk of an erring conscience: "In view of the quality of conscience as such, there is no sense in speaking of error, because there is no higher observation point from which error could be ascertained" (136). Why not? Is there no truth concerning the good [that is] accessible to all of us in common? To be sure, the point is then so significantly nuanced that finally, in the end, it is even less clear to me why the concept of the erring conscience should be untenable. Helpful here is M. Honecker, *Einführung in die theologische Ethik* (Berlin: 1990), 138ff.

like to pursue this question, not in the form of a strictly conceptual and therefore unavoidably abstract presentation, but by way of narrative, as one might say today—by relating, to begin with, the story of my own encounter with this problem.

I first became aware of the question with all its urgency in the beginning of my academic teaching. In the course of a dispute, a senior colleague, who was keenly aware of the plight of being Christian in our times, expressed the opinion that one should actually be grateful to God that he allows there to be so many unbelievers in good conscience. For if their eyes were opened and they became believers, they would not be capable, in this world of ours, of bearing the burden of faith with all its moral obligations. But as it is, since they can go another way in good conscience, they can still reach salvation.

What shocked me about this assertion was not in the first place the idea of an erroneous conscience given by God himself in order to save men by means of such artfulness— the idea, so to speak, of a blindness sent by God for the salvation of those in question. What disturbed me was the notion it harbored that faith is a burden that can hardly be borne and that was, no doubt, intended only for stronger natures—faith almost as a kind of punishment—in any case, an imposition not easily coped with.

According to this view, faith would not make salvation easier but harder. Being happy would mean not being burdened with having to believe or having to submit to the moral yoke of the faith of the Catholic Church. The erroneous conscience, which makes life easier and marks a more human course, would then be the real grace, the normal way to salvation. Untruth, keeping truth at bay, would be better for man than truth. It would not be the truth that would set him free, but rather he would have to be freed from the truth. Man would be more at home in the dark than in the light. Faith would not be the good gift of the good God but instead an affliction.

If this were the state of affairs, how could faith give rise to joy? Who would have the courage to pass faith on to others? Would it not be better to spare them the truth or even keep them from it? In the last few decades, notions of this sort have discernibly crippled the disposition to evangelize. The one who sees the faith as a heavy burden or as a moral imposition is unable to invite others to believe. Rather, he lets them be, in the putative freedom of their good consciences.

The one who spoke in this manner was a sincere believer and, I would say, a strict Catholic, who performed his moral duty with care and conviction. But he expressed a form of experience of faith that is disquieting. Its propagation could only be fatal to the faith. The almost traumatic aversion many have to what they hold to be "preconciliar" Catholicism is rooted, I am convinced, in the encounter with such a faith, seen only as an encumbrance. In this regard, to be sure, some very basic questions arise. Can such a faith actually be an encounter with truth? Is the truth about *God* and man so sad and difficult, or does truth not lie in the overcoming of such legalism? Does it not lie in freedom? But where does freedom lead? What course does it chart for us?

At the conclusion, we shall come back to these fundamental problems of Christian existence today, but before we do that, we must return to the core of our topic, namely, the matter of conscience. As I said, what unsettled me in the argument just recounted was first of all the caricature of faith I perceived in it. In a second course of reflection, it occurred to me further that the concept of conscience that it implied must also be wrong.

The erroneous conscience, by sheltering the person from the exacting demands of truth, saves him—thus went the argument. Conscience does not appear here as a window through which one can see outward to that common truth which founds and sustains us all and so makes possible through the common recognition of truth the community of wants and responsibilities. Conscience here does not mean man's openness to the ground of his being, the power of perception for what is highest and most essential. Rather, it appears as subjectivity's protective shell, into which man can escape and there hide from reality.

Liberalism's idea of conscience was, in fact, presupposed here: conscience does not open the way to the redemptive road to truth—which either does not exist or, if it does, is too demanding. It is the faculty that dispenses with truth. It thereby becomes the justification for subjectivity, which would not like to have itself called into question. Similarly, it becomes the justification for social conformity. As the mediating value between the different subjectivities, social conformity is intended to make living together possible. The obligation to seek the truth terminates, as do any doubts about the general inclination of society and what it has become accustomed to. Being convinced of oneself, as well as conforming to others, is sufficient. Man is reduced to his superficial conviction, and the less depth he has, the better for him.

What I was only dimly aware of in this conversation became glaringly clear a little later in a dispute among colleagues about the justifying power of the erroneous conscience. Objecting to this thesis, someone countered that if this were so, then the Nazi SS would be justified and we should seek them in heaven, since they carried out all their atrocities with fanatic conviction and complete certainty of conscience. Another colleague responded with utmost assurance that, of course, this was indeed the case: there is no doubting the fact that Hitler and his accomplices, who were deeply convinced of their cause, could not have acted otherwise. Therefore, the objective terribleness of their deeds notwithstanding, they acted morally, subjectively speaking. Since they followed their (albeit mistaken) consciences, one would have to recognize their conduct as moral and, as a result, should not doubt their eternal salvation.

After that conversation, I knew with complete certainty that something was wrong with the theory of the justifying power of the subjective conscience—that, in other words, a concept of conscience that leads to such results must be false. Firm, subjective conviction and the lack of doubts and scruples that follow from it do not justify man.

Some thirty years later, in the terse words of psychologist Albert Görres, I found summarized the perceptions I was trying to articulate. The elaboration of his insights forms the heart of this address. Görres shows that the feeling of guilt, the capacity to recognize guilt, belongs essentially to the spiritual make-up of man. This feeling of guilt disturbs the false calm of conscience and could be called conscience's complaint against my self-satisfied existence. It is as necessary for man as the physical pain that signifies disturbances of normal bodily functioning. Whoever is no longer capable of perceiving guilt is spiritually ill, "a living corpse, a dramatic character's mask", as Görres says.[10]

"Monsters, among other brutes, are the ones without guilt feelings. Perhaps Hitler did not have any, or Himmler, or Stalin. Maybe Mafia bosses do not have any guilt feelings, either, or maybe their remains are just well hidden

---

[10] A. Görres, "Schuld und Schuldgefahle", *Internationale katholische Zeitschrift "Communio"* 13 (1984): 434.

in the cellar. Even aborted guilt feelings.... All men need guilt feelings."[11]

By the way, a look into Sacred Scripture should have precluded such diagnoses and such a theory of justification by the errant conscience. In Psalm 19:12–13, we find the ever-worth-pondering passage, "But who can discern his errors? Clear me from hidden faults." That is not Old Testament objectivism, but the most profound human wisdom. No longer seeing one's guilt, the falling silent of conscience in so many areas is an even more dangerous sickness of the soul than the guilt that one still recognizes as such. He who no longer notices that killing is a sin has fallen farther than the one who still recognizes the shamefulness of his actions, because the former is further removed from the truth and conversion.

Not without reason does the self-righteous man in the encounter with Jesus appear as the one who is really lost. If the tax collector with all his undisputed sins stands more justified before God than the Pharisee with all his undeniably good works (Lk 18:9–14), this is not because the sins of the tax collector were not sins or because the good deeds of the Pharisee were not good deeds. Nor does it mean that the good that man does is not good before God, or the evil, not evil or at least not particularly important.

The reason for this paradoxical judgment of God is shown precisely from our question. The Pharisee no longer knows that he, too, has guilt. He has a completely clear conscience. But this silence of conscience makes him impenetrable to God and men, while the cry of conscience that plagues the tax collector makes him capable of truth and love. Jesus can move sinners. Not hiding behind the screen of their erroneous consciences, they have not

---

[11] Ibid., 442.

become unreachable for the change that God expects of them—of us. He is ineffective with the "righteous" because they are not aware of any need for forgiveness and conversion. Their consciences no longer accuse them but justify them.

We find something similar in Saint Paul, who tells us that the pagans, even without the law, knew quite well what God expected of them (Rom 2:1–16). The whole theory of salvation through ignorance breaks apart with this verse: there is present in man the truth, which is not to be repulsed—that one truth of the Creator, which in the revelation of salvation history has also been put in writing. Man can see the truth of God from the fact of his creaturehood. Not to see it is guilt. It is not seen because man does not want to see it. The "no" of the will that hinders recognition is guilt. The fact that the signal lamp does not shine is the consequence of a deliberate looking away from that which we do not wish to see.[12]

At this point in our reflections, it is possible to draw some initial conclusions with a view toward answering the question regarding the essence of conscience. We can now say that it will not do to identify man's conscience with the self-consciousness of the "I", with its subjective certainty about itself and its moral behavior. On the one hand, this consciousness may be a mere reflection of the social surroundings and the opinions in circulation. On the other hand, it might also derive from a lack of self-criticism, a deficiency in listening to the depths of one's own soul.

This diagnosis is confirmed by what has come to light since the fall of Marxist systems in Eastern Europe. The noblest and keenest minds of the liberated peoples speak of an enormous spiritual devastation that appeared in the

[12] See Honecker, *Einführung in die theologische Ethik*, 130.

years of the intellectual deformation. They speak of a blunting of the moral sense, which is a more significant loss and danger than the economic damage that was done.

The new patriarch of Moscow stressed this poignantly in the summer of 1990. The power of perception of people who lived in a system of deception was darkened. The society lost the capacity for mercy, and human feelings were forsaken. A whole generation was lost for the good, lost for humane deeds. "We must lead society back to the eternal moral values", that is to say, open ears almost gone deaf, so that once again the promptings of God might be heard in human hearts. Error, the "erring" conscience, is only at first convenient. But then the silencing of conscience leads to the dehumanization of the world and to moral danger if one does not work against it.

To put it differently, the identification of conscience with superficial consciousness, the reduction of man to his subjectivity, does not liberate but enslaves. It makes us totally dependent on the prevailing opinions and debases these with every passing day. Whoever equates conscience with superficial conviction identifies conscience with a pseudo-rational certainty, a certainty that in fact has been woven from self-righteousness, conformity, and lethargy. Conscience is degraded to a mechanism for *rationalization*, while it should represent the transparency of the subject for the divine and, thus, constitute the very dignity and greatness of man.

The reduction of conscience to subjective certitude betokens at the same time a retreat from truth. When the psalmist in anticipation of Jesus' view of sin and justice pleads for liberation from unconscious guilt, he points to the following relation: certainly, one must follow an erroneous conscience. But the departure from truth that took place beforehand and now takes its revenge is the actual guilt, which first lulls man into false security and then abandons him in the trackless waste.

b. Newman and Socrates: Guides to Conscience

At this juncture, I would like to make a temporary digression. Before we attempt to formulate reasonable answers to the questions regarding the essence of conscience, we must first widen the basis of our considerations somewhat, going beyond the personal, which has thus far constituted our point of departure. To be sure, my purpose is not to try to develop a scholarly study on the history of theories of conscience, a subject on which different contributions have appeared just recently in fact.[13] I would prefer, rather, to stay with our approach thus far of example and narrative.

A first glance should be directed to Cardinal Newman, whose life and work could be designated a single great commentary on the question of conscience. Nor should Newman be treated in a technical way. The given framework does not permit us to weigh the particulars of Newman's concept of conscience. I would simply like to try to indicate the place of conscience in the whole of Newman's life and thought. The insights gained from this will hopefully sharpen our view of present problems and establish the link to history, that is, both to the great witnesses of conscience and to the origin of the Christian doctrine of living according to conscience.

[13] Besides the important article of Reiner and the work of Schockenhoff on new studies (already cited), see A. Laun, *Das Gewissen: Oberste Norm sittlichen Handelns* (Innsbruck, Austria: 1984) and his *Aktuelle Probleme der Moraltheologie* (Vienna, Austria: 1991), 31–64; J. Gründel, ed., *Das Gewissen: Subjektive Willkür oder oberste Norm?* (Düsseldorf, 1990); and a summary overview, "Gewissen", by K. Golser, in H. Rotter and G. Virt, eds., *Neues Lexikon der christlichen Moral* (Innsbruck, Austria: Tyrölia, 1990), 278–86.

When the subject of Newman and conscience is raised, the famous sentence from his letter to the Duke of Norfolk immediately comes to mind: "Certainly, if I am obliged to bring religion into after-dinner toasts, (which indeed does not seem quite the thing), I shall drink—to the Pope, if you please,—still, to Conscience first, and to the Pope afterwards."[14]

In contrast to the statements of Gladstone, Newman sought to make a clear avowal of the papacy. And in contrast to mistaken forms of ultra-Montanism, Newman embraced an interpretation of the papacy, which is only then correctly conceived when it is viewed together with the primacy of conscience—a papacy not put in opposition to the primacy of conscience but based on it and guaranteeing it. Modern man, who presupposes the opposition of authority to subjectivity, has difficulty understanding this.

For him, conscience stands on the side of subjectivity and is the expression of the freedom of the subject. Authority, on the other hand, appears to him as the constraint on, threat to, and even negation of freedom. So, then, we must go deeper to recover a vision in which this kind of opposition does not obtain.

For Newman, the middle term—which establishes the connection between authority and subjectivity—is truth. I do not hesitate to say that truth is the central thought of Newman's intellectual grappling. Conscience is central for him because truth stands in the middle. To put it differently, the centrality of the concept *conscience* for Newman is linked to the prior centrality of the concept *truth*

[14] Newman to the Duke of Norfolk, December 27, 1874, in *The Works of Cardinal Newman: Difficulties of Anglicans*, vol. 2 (Westminster, Md.: Christian Classics, 1969), 261; see J. Honore, *Newman: Sa Vie et sa pensée* (Paris: 1988), 65, and I. Ker, *John Henry Newman: A Biography* (Oxford: Oxford University Press, 1990), 688ff.

and can only be understood from this vantage point. The dominance of the idea of conscience in Newman does not signify that he, in the nineteenth century and in contrast to "objectivistic" neo-scholasticism, espoused a philosophy or theology of subjectivity. Certainly, the subject finds in Newman an attention that it had not received in Catholic theology perhaps since Saint Augustine. But it is an attention in the line of Augustine and not in that of the subjectivist philosophy of the modern age.

On the occasion of his elevation to cardinal, Newman declared that most of his life had been a struggle against the spirit of liberalism in religion; we might add, also against Christian subjectivism, as he found it in the Evangelical movement of his time, which admittedly had provided him the first step on his lifelong road to conversion.[15]

Conscience for Newman does not mean that the subject is the standard vis-à-vis the claims of authority in a truthless world, a world that lives with a compromise between the claims of the subject and the claims of the social order. Much more than that, conscience signifies the perceptible and demanding presence of the voice of truth in the subject himself. It is the overcoming of mere subjectivity in the encounter of the inferiority of man with the truth from *God*. The verse Newman composed in 1833 in Sicily is characteristic: "I loved to choose and see my path; but now lead thou me on!"[16]

Newman's conversion to Catholicism was not for him a matter of personal taste or of subjective, spiritual need.

[15] See C. Dessain, *John Henry Newman: A Biography*, 3rd ed. (Oxford: Oxford University Press, 1980); and G. Biemer, *John Henry Newman: Leben und Werk* (Mainz: Grünewald, 1989).

[16] From the famous poem "Lead Kindly Light", in Newman, *Verses on Various Occasions* (London: Longmans, 1888); cf. Ker, *Newman*, 79, and Dessain, *Newman*, 33–34.

He expressed himself on this even in 1844, on the threshold, so to speak, of his conversion: "No one can have a more unfavorable view than I of the present state of the Roman Catholics."[17] Newman was much more taken by the necessity to obey recognized truth than his own preferences, that is to say, even against his own sensitivity and bonds of friendship and ties due to similar backgrounds. It seems to me characteristic of Newman that he emphasized truth's priority over goodness in the order of virtues. Or, to put it in a way that is more understandable for us, he emphasized truth's priority over consensus, over the accommodation of groups.

I would say, when we are speaking of a man of conscience, we mean one who looks at things this way. A man of conscience is one who never acquires tolerance, well-being, success, public standing, and approval on the part of prevailing opinion at the expense of truth. In this regard, Newman is related to Britain's other great witness of conscience, Thomas More, for whom conscience was not at all an expression of subjective stubbornness or obstinate heroism. He numbered himself, in fact, among those fainthearted martyrs who only after faltering and much questioning succeed in mustering up obedience to conscience, mustering up obedience to the truth, which must stand higher than any human tribunal or any type of personal taste.[18]

Thus, two standards become apparent for ascertaining the presence of a real voice of conscience. First, conscience is not identical to personal wishes and taste.

---

[17] Newman to J. Keble, December 29, 1844, in *Correspondence of J. H. Newman with J. Keble and Others: 1839–1845* (London: 1917), 364; see also 351 and Dessain, *Newman*, 79.

[18] See P. Berglar, *Die Stunde des Thomas Morus*, 3rd ed. (Ölten, Switzerland: Walter, 1981), 155ff.

Second, conscience cannot be reduced to social advantage, to group consensus, or to the demands of political and social power.

Let us take a side look now at the situation of our day. The individual may not achieve his advancement or well-being at the cost of betraying what he recognizes to be true; nor may mankind. Here we come in contact with the really critical issue of the modern age. The concept of truth has been virtually given up and replaced by the concept of progress. Progress itself "is" the truth. But through this seeming exaltation, progress loses its direction and becomes nullified. For if no direction exists, everything can just as well be regress as progress.

Einstein's relativity theory properly concerns the physical cosmos. But it seems to me to describe exactly the situation of the intellectual and spiritual world of our time. Relativity theory states that there are no fixed systems of reference in the universe. When we declare a system to be a reference point from which we try to measure the whole, it is we who do the determining. Only in such a way can we attain any results at all. But the determination could always have been done differently.

What we said about the physical cosmos is reflected in the second "Copernican revolution" regarding our basic relationship to reality. The truth as such, the absolute, the very reference point of thinking, is no longer visible. For this reason, precisely in the spiritual sense, there is no longer "up or down". There are no directions in a world without fixed measuring points. What we view to be direction is based, not on a standard that is true in itself, but on our decision and, finally, on considerations of expediency. In such a "relativistic" context, so-called ideological or consequentialist ethics ultimately becomes nihilistic, even if it fails to see this. And what is called conscience in such a world view is, on deeper reflection, but a euphemistic way of saying that there is no such thing as an actual conscience, conscience understood as a "co-knowing" with the truth. Each person determines his own standards. And, needless to say, in general relativity, no one can be of much help to the other, much less prescribe behavior to him.

At this point, the whole radicality of today's dispute over ethics and conscience, its center, becomes plain. It seems to me that the parallel in the history of thought is the quarrel between Socrates-Plato and the Sophists, in which the fateful decision between two fundamental positions has been rehearsed. There is, on the one hand, the position of confidence in man's capacity for truth. On the other, there is a world view in which man alone sets the standards for himself.[19] The fact that Socrates, the pagan, could become in a certain respect the prophet of Jesus Christ has its roots in this fundamental question. Socrates' taking up of this question bestowed on the way of philosophizing inspired by him a kind of salvation-historical privilege and made it an appropriate vessel for the Christian Logos. For with the Christian Logos we are dealing with liberation through truth and to truth.

If you isolate Socrates' dispute from the accidents of the time and take into account his use of other arguments and terminology, you begin to see how much his is the same dilemma we face today. Giving up the idea of man's capacity for truth leads first to pure formalism in the use

---

[19] Regarding the debate between Socrates and the Sophists, see J. Pieper, "Missbrauch der Sprache—Missbrauch der Macht", in *Über die Schwierigkeit, heute zu glauben* (Munich: 1974), 255–82; and *Kümmert euch nicht um Sokrates* (Munich, 1966). A penetrating treatment of the question of the truth as the center of Socratic searching is found in R. Guardini, *The Death of Socrates* (New York, 1948).

of words and concepts. Again, the loss of content, then and now, leads to a pure formalism of judgment. In many places today, for example, no one bothers any longer to ask what a person thinks. The verdict on someone's thinking is ready at hand as long as you can assign it to its corresponding, formal category: conservative, reactionary, fundamentalist, progressive, revolutionary. Assignment to a formal scheme suffices to render unnecessary coming to terms with the content. *what it is actually*

The same thing can be seen in more concentrated form in art. What a work of art says is indifferent. It can glorify God or the devil. The sole standard is that of formal, technical mastery.

We have now arrived at the heart of the matter. Where contents no longer count, where pure praxeology takes over, technique becomes the highest criterion. This means, though, that power becomes the preeminent category, whether revolutionary or reactionary. This is precisely the distorted form of being-like-God of which the account of the Fall speaks. The way of mere technical skill, the way of sheer power, is imitation of an idol and not expression of one's being made in the image and likeness of God. What characterizes man as man is that he asks, not about the "can", but about the "should" and that he opens himself to the voice and demands of truth.

It seems to me that this was the final meaning of the Socratic search, and it is the most profound element in the witness of all martyrs. They attest to the fact that man's capacity for truth is a limit on all power and a guarantee of man's likeness to God. It is precisely in this way that the martyrs are the great witnesses of conscience, of that capability given to man to perceive the "should" beyond the "can" and thereby render possible real progress, real ascent.

c. Systematic Consequences: The Two Levels of Conscience

Anamnesis

After all these ramblings through intellectual history, it is finally time to arrive at some conclusions, that is, to formulate a concept of conscience. The medieval tradition was right, I believe, in according two levels to the concept of conscience. These levels, though they can be well distinguished, must be continually referred to each other.[20] It seems to me that many unacceptable theses regarding conscience are the result of neglecting either the difference or the connection between the two. Mainstream scholasticism expressed these two levels in the concepts *synderesis* and *conscientia*.

The word *synderesis* (*synteresis*) came into the medieval tradition of conscience from the Stoic doctrine of the microcosm.[21] It remained unclear in its exact meaning and, for this reason, became a hindrance to a careful development of this essential aspect of the whole question of conscience. I would like, therefore, without entering into philosophical disputes, to replace this problematic word with the much more clearly defined Platonic concept of anamnesis. Not only is it linguistically clearer and philosophically deeper and purer, but anamnesis above all also harmonizes with key motifs of biblical thought and the anthropology derived from it.

The word *anamnesis* should be taken to mean exactly that which Paul expressed in the second chapter of his Letter to the Romans: "When Gentiles who have not the

---

[20] A short summary of the medieval doctrine of conscience can be found in Reiner, "Gewissen", 582–83.

[21] See E. von Ivanka, *Plato Christianus* (Einsiedeln: Johannes Verlag, 1964), 315–51, especially 320–21.

law do by nature what the law requires, they are a law to themselves, even though they do not have the law. They show that what the law requires is written on their hearts, while their conscience also bears witness" (2:14–15).

The same thought is strikingly amplified in the great monastic rule of Saint Basil. Here we read: The love of God is not founded on a discipline imposed on us from outside but is constitutively established in us as the capacity and necessity of our rational nature.

Basil speaks in terms of "the spark of divine love that has been hidden in us", an expression that was to become important in medieval mysticism.[22] In the spirit of Johannine theology, Basil knows that love consists in keeping the commandments. For this reason, the spark of love, which has been put into us by the Creator, means this: "We have received interiorly beforehand the capacity and disposition for observing all divine commandments.... These are not something imposed from without." Referring everything back to its simple core, Augustine adds, "We could never judge that one thing is better than another if a basic understanding of the good had not already been instilled in us."[23]

This means that the first so-called ontological level of the phenomenon conscience consists in the fact that something like an original memory of the good and true (they are identical) has been implanted in us, that there is an inner ontological tendency within man, who is created in the likeness of God, toward the divine. From its origin, man's being resonates with some things and clashes with others. This anamnesis of the origin, which results from the godlike constitution of our being, is not a conceptually articulated knowing, a store of retrievable contents. It is,

[22] Basil, *Regulae fusius tractatae*, Resp. 2, 1: *PG* 31:908.
[23] Augustine, *De Trinitate* VIII, 3 (4), *PL* 42:949.

so to speak, an inner sense, a capacity to recall, so that the one whom it addresses, if he is not turned in on himself, hears its echo from within. He sees: That's it! That is what my nature points to and seeks.

The possibility for and right to mission rest on this anamnesis of the Creator, which is identical to the ground of our existence. The Gospel may, indeed must, be proclaimed to the pagans, because they themselves are yearning for it in the hidden recesses of their souls (see Is 42:4). Mission is vindicated, then, when those addressed recognize in the encounter with the word of the Gospel that this indeed is what they have been waiting for.

In this sense, Paul can say that the Gentiles are a law to themselves—not in the sense of the modern liberal notions of autonomy, which preclude transcendence of the subject, but in the much deeper sense that nothing belongs less to me than I myself. My own "I" is the site of the most profound surpassing of self and contact with him from whom I came and toward whom I am going.

In these sentences, Paul expresses the experience that he had had as missionary to the Gentiles and that Israel may have experienced before him in dealings with the "god-fearing". Israel could have experienced among the Gentiles what the ambassadors of Jesus Christ found reconfirmed. Their proclamation answered an expectation. Their proclamation encountered an antecedent basic knowledge of the essential constants of the will of God, which came to be written down in the commandments, which can be found in all cultures, and which can be all the more clearly elucidated the less an overbearing cultural bias distorts this primordial knowledge. The more man lives in "fear of the Lord" (consider the story of Cornelius, especially Acts 10:34–35), the more concretely and clearly effective this anamnesis becomes.

Again, let us take a formulation of Saint Basil. The love of God, which is concrete in the commandments, is not imposed on us from without, the Church Father emphasizes, but has been implanted in us beforehand. The sense for the good has been stamped upon us, as Augustine puts it. We can now appreciate Newman's toast first to conscience and then to the pope. The pope cannot impose commandments on faithful Catholics because he wants to or finds it expedient. Such a modern, voluntaristic concept of authority can only distort the true theological meaning of the papacy. The true nature of the Petrine office has become so incomprehensible in the modern age no doubt because we think of authority only in terms that do not allow for bridges between subject and object. Accordingly, everything that does not come from the subject is thought to be externally imposed.

But the situation is really quite different according to the anthropology of conscience, of which we have tried to come to an appreciation in these reflections. The anamnesis instilled in our being needs, one might say, assistance from without so that it can become aware of itself. But this "from without" is not something set in opposition to anamnesis but is ordered to it. It has a maieutic function, imposes nothing foreign, but brings to fruition what is proper to anamnesis, namely, its interior openness to the truth.

When we are dealing with the question of faith and Church, whose radius extends from the redeeming Logos over the gift of creation, we must, however, take into account yet another dimension, which is especially developed in the Johannine writings. John is familiar with the anamnesis of the new "we", which is granted to us in the incorporation into Christ (one body, that is, one "I" with him). In remembering, they knew him, as the Gospel has it in a number of places.

The original encounter with Jesus gave the disciples what all generations thereafter receive in their foundational encounter with the Lord in baptism and the Eucharist, namely, the new anamnesis of faith, which unfolds, like the anamnesis of creation, in constant dialogue between *within* and *without*. In contrast to the presumption of Gnostic teachers, who wanted to convince the faithful that their naïve faith must be understood and applied much differently, John could say, You do not need such instruction; as anointed ones (baptized ones), you know everything (see 1 Jn 2:20).

This does not mean a factual omniscience on the part of the faithful. It does signify, however, the sureness of the Christian memory. This Christian memory, to be sure, is always learning, but, proceeding from its sacramental identity, it also distinguishes *from within* between what is a genuine unfolding of its recollection and what is its destruction or falsification. In the crisis of the Church today, the power of this recollection and the truth of the apostolic word are experienced in an entirely new way, where (much more so than hierarchical direction) it is the power of memory of the simple faith that leads to the discernment of spirits.

One can comprehend the primacy of the pope and its correlation to Christian conscience only in this connection. The true sense of the teaching authority of the pope consists in his being the advocate of the Christian memory. The pope does not impose from without. Rather, he elucidates the Christian memory and defends it. For this reason, the toast to conscience indeed must precede the toast to the pope, because without conscience there would not be a papacy. All power that the papacy has is power of conscience. It is service to the double memory on which the faith is based—and which again and again must be purified, expanded, and defended against the destruction of memory that is threatened by a subjectivity forgetful of its own foundation, as well as by the pressures of social and cultural conformity.

Conscientia

Having considered this first, essentially ontological level of the concept of conscience, we must now turn to its second level—that of judgment and decision, which the medieval tradition designates with the single word *conscientia*, conscience. Presumably this terminological tradition has not insignificantly contributed to the diminution of the concept of conscience. Saint Thomas, for example, designates only this second level as *conscientia*. For him, it stands to reason that conscience is not a *habitus*, that is, a lasting ontic quality of man, but *actus*, an event in execution. Thomas, of course, assumes as given the ontological foundation of anamnesis (*synderesis*). He describes anamnesis as an inner repugnance to evil and attraction to the good.

The act of conscience applies this basic knowledge to the particular situation. It is divided, according to Thomas, into three elements: recognizing (*recognoscere*), bearing witness (*testificari*), and, finally, judging (*iudicare*). One might speak of an interaction between a function of control and a function of decision.[24] Thomas sees this sequence according to the Aristotelian tradition's model of deductive reasoning. But he is careful to emphasize what is peculiar to this knowledge of moral actions whose conclusions do not come from mere knowing or thinking.[25]

Whether something is recognized or not depends, too, on the will, which can block the way to recognition or

---

[24] See Reiner, "Gewissen", 582; Aquinas, *Summa Theologiae* I, q. 79, a. 13; and Aquinas, *De Ver.*, q. 17, a. 1.

[25] See the careful study of L. Melina, *La conoscenza morale: Linee di riflessione sul commento di San Tommaso all'Etica Nicomachea* (Rome: Città Nuova Editrice, 1987), 69ff.

lead to it. It is dependent, that is to say, on an already formed moral character, which can either continue to deform or be further purified.[26] On this level, the level of judgment (*conscientia* in the narrower sense), it can be said that even the erroneous conscience binds. This statement is completely intelligible from the rational tradition of scholasticism. No one may act against his convictions, as Saint Paul had already said (Rom 14:23). But this fact—that the conviction a person has come to certainly binds in the moment of acting—does not signify a canonization of subjectivity. It is never wrong to follow the convictions one has arrived at—in fact, one must do so. But it can very well be wrong to have come to such askew convictions in the first place by having stifled the protest of the anamnesis of being.

The guilt lies, then, in a different place, much deeper—not in the present act, not in the present judgment of conscience, but in the neglect of my being that made me deaf to the internal promptings of truth.[27] For this reason,

[26] In reflecting on his own inner experience in the decades following his conversion, St. Augustine elaborated fundamental insights into the essence of freedom and morality concerning the relationships between knowledge, will, emotion, and inclination through habit. See the excellent presentation of P. Brown, *Augustine of Hippo: A Biography* (New York: Dorset, 1986), 146–57.

[27] That this precisely is also the position of St. Thomas Aquinas is shown by I. G. Belmans in his extremely enlightening study, "Le paradoxe de la conscience erronée d'Abélard à Karl Rahner", *Revue Thomiste* 90 (1990): 570–86. He shows how, with the publication of Sertillanges' book on St. Thomas in 1942, a then widely adopted distortion of Thomas' doctrine of conscience takes hold, which—to put it simply—consists in the fact that only the *Summa Theologiae* I–II, q. 19, a. 5 ("Must one follow an erroneous conscience?") is cited, and the following article, a. 6 ("Is it sufficient to follow one's conscience in order to act properly?"), is simply ignored. That means imputing the doctrine of Abelard to Thomas, whose goal was in fact to overcome Abelard. Abelard had taught that the crucifiers of Christ would not have sinned if they had acted from ignorance. The only way to sin consists in acting against conscience. The modern theories of the autonomy of conscience can appeal to Abelard but not to Thomas.

criminals of conviction like Hitler and Stalin are guilty. These crass examples should not serve to put us at ease but should rouse us to take seriously the earnestness of the plea, "Clear me from hidden faults" (Ps 19:12).

d. Epilogue: Conscience and Grace

At the end, there remains the question with which we began: Is not the truth, at least as the faith of the Church shows it to us, too lofty and difficult for man? Taking into consideration everything we have said, we can respond as follows:

Certainly, the high road to truth and goodness is not a comfortable one. It challenges man. Nevertheless, retreat into self, however comfortable, does not redeem. The self withers away and becomes lost. But in ascending the heights of the good, man discovers more and more the beauty that lies in the arduousness of truth, which constitutes redemption for him.

But not everything has yet been said. We would dissolve Christianity into moralism if no message that surpasses our own actions became discernible. Without many words, an image from the Greek world can show us this. In it we can observe simultaneously both how the anamnesis of the Creator extends from within us outward toward the Redeemer and how everyone may see him as Redeemer, because he answers our own innermost expectations.

I am speaking of the story of the expiation of Orestes' sin of matricide. Orestes had committed the murder as an act of conscience. This is designated by the mythological language of obedience to the command of the god Apollo. But now Orestes finds himself hounded by the Furies, or *Erinyes*, who are mythological personifications of conscience and who, from a deeper wellspring of recollection, reproach him, declaring that his decision of conscience, his obedience to the "saying of the gods", was in reality guilt. The whole tragedy of man comes to light in this dispute of the "gods", that is to say, in this conflict of conscience. In the holy court, the white stone of Athena leads to Orestes' acquittal, his sanctification, in the power of which the *Erinyes* are transformed into *Eumenides*, the spirits of reconciliation. Atonement has transformed the world.

The myth, while representing the transition from a system of blood vengeance to the right order of community, signifies much more than just that. Hans Urs von Balthasar expressed this "more" as follows: "Calming grace always assists in the establishing of justice, not the old graceless justice of the *Erinyes* period, but that which is full of grace."[28] This myth speaks to us of the human longing that conscience's objectively just indictment—and the attendant destructive, interior distress it causes in man— not be the last word. It thus speaks of an authority of grace, a power of expiation that allows the guilt to vanish and makes truth at last truly redemptive. It is the longing for a truth that does not just make demands of us but also transforms us through expiation and pardon. Through these, as Aeschylus puts it, "guilt is washed away",[29] and our being is transformed from within, beyond our own capability.

This is the real innovation of Christianity: the Logos, the truth in person, is also the atonement, the transforming forgiveness that is above and beyond our capability and incapability. Therein lies the real novelty on which the larger Christian memory is founded and that indeed, at the same time, constitutes the deeper answer to what the anamnesis of the Creator expects of us.

[28] Hans Urs von Balthasar, *Glory of the Lord: A Theological Aesthetics*, vol. 4: *The Realm of Metaphysics in Antiquity* (San Francisco: Ignatius Press, 1989), 121.

[29] Aeschylus, *Eumenides*, 2nd ed., ed. G. Murray (Oxford: Oxford University Press, 1955), 280–81; von Balthasar, *Glory of the Lord* 4:121.

Where this center of the Christian message is not sufficiently expressed and appreciated, truth becomes a yoke that is too heavy for our shoulders, from which we must seek to free ourselves. But the freedom gained thereby is empty. It leads into the desolate land of nothingness and disintegrates of itself. Yet the yoke of truth in fact became "easy" (Mt 11:30) when the Truth came, loved us, and consumed our guilt in the fire of his love. Only when we know and experience this from within will we be free to hear the message of conscience with joy and without fear.

3. THE SIGNIFICANCE OF ETHICAL AND RELIGIOUS VALUES IN A PLURALISTIC SOCIETY

a. Relativism as a Precondition of Democracy

Since the collapse of the totalitarian systems that left their mark on long stretches of the twentieth century, many people today have become convinced that, even if democracy does not bring about the ideal society, nevertheless it is in practice the only appropriate system of government. It brings about a distribution and control of power, thereby offering the greatest possible guarantee against despotism and oppression and ensuring the freedom of the individual and the maintenance of human rights. When we speak of democracy today, it is above all these good things that we have in mind. The participation of everyone in power is the hallmark of freedom. No one is to be merely the object of rule by others or only a person under control; everyone ought to be able to make a voluntary contribution to the

From Joseph Cardinal Ratzinger (Pope Benedict XVI), *Values in a Time of Upheaval*, trans. Brian McNeil (New York: Crossword; San Francisco: Ignatius Press, 2006), 53–72.

totality of political activity. We can all be free citizens only if we all have a genuine share in decision making.

The real goal of participation in power is thus universal freedom and equality. But since power cannot be continuously exercised in an immediate manner by everyone, it must be delegated for a period. And even if this transfer of power has a time limit (that is, until the next elections), it nevertheless requires controls in order that the common will of those who have handed over power remains determinative—for otherwise the will of those who exercise power might become independent from that of the voters. At this point, many would be inclined to call a halt in their reflections and say with satisfaction: if everyone's freedom is guaranteed, the state has reached its goal.

In this way, the freedom of the individual to order his own life is declared to be the real goal of societal life. Community has no value whatever in itself but exists only to allow the individual to be himself. However, if the individual freedom presented here as the highest goal lacks contents, it dissolves into thin air, since individual freedom can exist only when freedoms are correctly ordered. Individual freedom needs measure, for otherwise it turns into violence directed against others. It is not by chance that those who aim at totalitarian rule begin by introducing an anarchic freedom for individuals and a situation in which each one's hand is raised against all the others: by introducing order into this situation, they are enabled to present themselves as the true saviors of mankind. *Thus, freedom requires contents.* We can define it as the safeguarding of human rights, but we can also describe it more broadly as the guarantee that things will go well both with society and with the individual: the one who is ruled, that is, the one who has handed over power, "can be free when he recognizes himself, that is to say, his own good, in the common good that the rulers endeavor to bring about."[30]

This reflection has introduced two further concepts alongside the idea of freedom: law and the good. There exists a certain tension between freedom as the existential form of democracy and the contents of freedom (that is, law and the good), and contemporary struggles to discover the right form of democracy, and indeed of political life as a whole, are struggles to find the right balance in this tension.

Naturally, we tend to think of freedom as the true good of human beings; all other goods seem controversial today, since we feel that it is all too easy to abuse them. We do not want the state to impose one particular idea of the good on us. The problem becomes even clearer when we employ the concept of truth to clarify the concept of the good, since we think today that respect for the freedom of the individual makes it utterly wrong for the state to decide the question of truth—and this in turn means that we do not think it possible for a community as such to discern truth and, thus, truth about what is good. Truth is controversial, and the attempt to impose on all persons what one part of the citizenry holds to be true looks like the enslavement of people's consciences. The concept of "truth" has in fact moved into the zone of antidemocratic intolerance. It is not now a public good, but something private. It may perhaps be the good of specific groups, but it is not the truth of society as a whole. To make this point in other terms: the modern concept of democracy seems indissolubly linked to that of relativism. It is relativism that appears to be the real guarantee of freedom and especially of the very heart of human freedom, namely, freedom of religion and of conscience.

[30] H. Kuhn, *Der Staat: Eine philosophische Darstellung* (Munich, 1967), 60.

We would all agree on this today. Yet, if we look more closely, we are surely obliged to ask: Must there not be a nonrelativistic kernel in democracy, too? For is not democracy, ultimately constructed around human rights that are inviolable? Does not democracy appear necessary precisely in order to guarantee and protect these rights? Human rights are not subject to any demand for pluralism and tolerance: on the contrary, they *are* the very substance of tolerance and freedom. Law and freedom can never mean robbing another person of his rights. And this means that a basic element of truth, namely, ethical truth, is indispensable to democracy. We prefer today to speak of values rather than of truth, in order to avoid coming into conflict with the idea of tolerance and with democratic relativism. But such a terminological transposition will not allow us to evade the question I have just posed, since values derive their inviolability precisely from the fact that they are true and that they correspond to true requirements of human existence.

This makes a further question all the more urgent: What is the basis of these values that are valid in the community? Or, to use modern language: What is the basis of those fundamental values that are not subject to the interplay of the majority and the minority in society? How do we recognize them? What is not subject to relativism—and why and how is this the case?

This question is the center of contemporary debates in political philosophy, in our endeavor to achieve a genuine democracy. We could simplify somewhat and say that two basic positions are staked out; these are presented in a number of variants and sometimes even overlap. On the one hand, we find the radical relativistic position that wishes to eliminate the concept of the good (and thereby even more so the concept of that which is true) from politics altogether because it poses a risk to freedom. "Natural law" is rejected because it reeks of metaphysics. And this makes it possible to maintain a consistent relativism: there is ultimately no other principle governing political activity than the decision of the majority, which occupies the position of "truth" in the life of the state. Law can be understood only in purely political terms. In other words, law is whatever the competent organs of the state posit as law. Democracy, therefore, is not defined in terms of its contents, but in a purely functional manner, as a complex of rules that enable the construction of a majority, transfer of power, and change of government. Democracy consists essentially in the mechanisms of election and voting.

This view is opposed by a thesis that affirms that truth is not a product of politics (the majority) but is antecedent to political activity and sheds light on it. It is not praxis that creates truth but truth that makes praxis possible. Political activity is just and promotes freedom when it serves a complex of values and rights that reason makes known to us. The explicit skepticism of relativistic and positivistic theories is countered here by a basic confidence in the ability of human reason to make truth known.[31]

The essential character of these two positions can be seen very clearly in the trial of Jesus, when Pilate asks the Savior: "What is truth?" (Jn 18:38). One very prominent representative of the strictly relativistic position, the Austrian professor of jurisprudence Hans Kelsen, who later emigrated to America, has published a meditation on this biblical text in which he sets out his view with unmistakable clarity.[32]

---

[31] This fundamental question in the contemporary debate about the correct understanding of democracy is presented in a very illuminating manner in V. Possenti, *Le società liberali al bivio: Lineamenti di filosofia della società* (Genoa, 1991); see esp. 298ff.

[32] For details, see Possenti, *Le società liberali al bivio*, 315–45, and esp. 345f. On the debate with Kelsen, Kuhn, *Der Staat*, 41f., is also helpful.

We shall return below to Kelsen's political philosophy; let us first see how he expounds the biblical text.

Kelsen sees Pilate's question as an expression of the skepticism that a politician must possess. In this sense, the question is already an answer: truth is unattainable. And we see that this is indeed how Pilate thinks from the fact that he does not even wait for an answer from Jesus but turns immediately to address the crowd. He leaves it to the people to decide the disputed question by means of their vote. Kelsen holds that Pilate acts here as a perfect democrat: since he himself does not know what is just, he leaves it to the majority to decide. In this way, the Austrian scholar portrays Pilate as the emblematic figure of a relativistic and skeptical democracy that is based, not on values and truth, but on correct procedures. Kelsen seems not to be disturbed by the fact that the outcome of Jesus' trial was the condemnation of an innocent and righteous man. After all, there is no other truth than that of the majority, and one cannot "get behind" this truth to ask further questions. At one point, Kelsen even goes so far as to say that this relativistic certainty must be imposed, if need be, at the cost of blood and tears. One must be as certain of it as Jesus was certain of his own truth.[33]

The great exegete Heinrich Schlier offered a completely different exposition of this text, one that is much more convincing even from a political point of view. Schlier was writing in the period when National Socialism was preparing to seize power in Germany, and his exposition was a conscious testimony against those groups in the German Protestant churches who were willing to put "faith" and "people" on the same level.[34] Schlier points out that

[33] See Possenti, *Le società liberali al bivio*, 336.

[34] H. Schlier, "Die Beurteilung des Staates im Neuen Testament", first published in 1932 in *Zwischen den Zeiten*; quoted here from his collected essays: H. Schlier, *Die Zeit der Kirche*, 2nd ed. (Freiburg im Breisgau, 1958), 1–16; see also the essay "Jesus und Pilatus" in the same volume, 56–74.

although Jesus in his trial acknowledges the judicial authority of the state represented by Pilate, he also sets limits to
this authority by saying that Pilate does not possess this
authority on his own account but has it "from above"
(19:11). Pilate falsifies his power, and hence also the power
of the state, as soon as he ceases to exercise it as the faithful
administrator of a higher order that depends on truth and,
instead, exploits power to his own advantage. The governor no longer asks what truth is but understands power as
sheer, unadulterated power. "As soon as he legitimated his
own self, he became the instrument of the judicial murder
of Jesus."[35]

b. What Is the State for?

This demonstrates the questionable nature of a strictly
relativistic position. On the other hand, we are all aware
today of the problems entailed by a position that would
make truth fundamental and relevant to democratic praxis.
Fear of the Inquisition and the violation of conscience has
been too deeply etched in us. Is there any way out of this
dilemma? Let us begin by asking what the state in fact is.
What is it for, and what is it not for? We will then look at
the various answers that are given to these questions and,
finally, attempt to arrive at a concluding answer.

What is the state? What purpose does it serve? We could
quite simply affirm that it is the task of the state "to regu-
late human life in society",[36] creating a balance of freedom
and good things that allows each individual to lead a life
worthy of man. We could also say that the state guarantees
the law, which is a precondition of freedom and of shared
prosperity. Governance is an essential element of the state,
but this governance is not merely the exercise of power

[35] Schlier, Die Zeit der Kirche, 3.
[36] Ibid., 11.

but the safeguard of the rights of each individual and the welfare of all. It is not the task of the state to create mankind's happiness, nor is it the task of the state to create new men. It is not the task of the state to change the world into a paradise—nor can it do so. If it tries, it abandons its own boundaries and posits itself as something absolute. It behaves as if it were God, and, as the Revelation of John shows, this makes it the beast from the abyss, the power of the Antichrist.

In this context, we should always bear two scriptural texts in mind, Romans 13 and Revelation 13, which are only apparently antithetical. The Letter to the Romans describes the state in its ordered form, a state that keeps to its own proper boundaries and does not present itself as the source of truth and law. Paul envisages the state as the faithful custodian of good order, enabling people to live well as individuals and as a community. We must obey this state: obedience to the law does not prevent freedom but rather makes freedom possible. The Apocalypse paints a different picture: here, the state declares itself to be a god and determines autonomously what is to be counted as righteous and true. Such a state destroys man by denying his true being. It has therefore lost its claim on our obedience.[37]

It is significant that both National Socialism and Marxism basically denied the state and the law. They declared the bond of law to be servitude, claiming to replace it with something higher, the so-called "will of the people" or the "classless society", which was meant to take the place of the state (since the state was the instrument of the hegemony of one single class). In regarding the state and its ordered structures as the foe of the absolute

[37] See ibid., 3–7; 14–16.

claims made by their own ideology, these demagogues remained at least to some extent aware of what a state really is: the state establishes a relative ordering for life in society, but it cannot answer on its own the question of the meaning of human existence. Not only must it leave space open for something else, perhaps for something higher; it must also receive from outside itself the truth about what is right, since it does not bear this truth in itself. But how and where does this happen? It is time to investigate this question.

c. The Contradictory Answers to the Questions of the Foundations of Democracy

The Relativistic Theory

As I have said above, two diametrically opposed positions offer answers to these questions, but there are also intermediary views. We have already encountered the first view, that of a strict relativism, in the figure of Hans Kelsen. For him the relationship between religion and democracy is only negative, since one particular characteristic of Christianity is that it teaches absolute truths and values, and this is the exact antithesis of the necessary skepticism of a relativistic democracy. Kelsen understands religion as a heteronomy of the person, whereas democracy retains the autonomy of the person. This also means that the core of democracy is freedom, not the good, for that is something that puts freedom at risk.[38] Today, the American legal philosopher Richard Rorty is the best-known representative of this view of democracy. His version of the connection between democracy and relativism expresses to a large extent the average awareness even of Christians today and

---

[38] See Possenti, *Le società liberali al bivio*, 321.

therefore deserves close attention. Rorty argues that the only criterion for the formulation of law is the widespread conviction held by the majority of the citizens. Democracy does not have access to any other philosophy or any other source of law. Naturally, Rorty is aware that it is ultimately unsatisfactory to appeal to the majority principle as the only source of truth. We see this from his affirmation that pragmatic reason that is orientated to the majority will always include a number of intuitive ideas, such as the rejection of slavery.[39] Here, of course, he is mistaken: for centuries, or even millennia, the sensitivities of the majority did not include this particular intuition, and no one can predict how long the majority will in fact reject slavery. Here we see an empty concept of freedom that can even maintain that the dissolution of the ego, so that it becomes a phenomenon without a center and without an essence, is necessary in order specifically to shape our intuition about the preeminence of freedom. But what if this intuition disappears? What if a majority forms against freedom and tells us that man is not mature enough for freedom but wants and ought to be led?

There is certainly something enticing in the idea that only the majority can make decisions in a democracy and that the only source of law can be those convictions held by citizens who are capable of assembling majority support. For whenever the majority is obliged to accept something that is not willed and decided by this majority, it seems that its freedom is denied and therefore the very essence of democracy is denied. Every other theory appears to assume a dogmatism that undermines self-determination, depriving citizens of the right to make decisions and abolishing their freedom.

[39] Ibid., 293.

On the other hand, one can scarcely deny that the majority is capable of making mistakes. These errors do not concern only peripheral matters. They can call fundamental goods into question so that human dignity and human rights are no longer guaranteed and freedom loses its very raison d'être. It is certainly not always clear to the majority what human rights are or what human dignity really implies. The history of the twentieth century offers dramatic proof that majorities can be seduced and manipulated and that freedom can be destroyed precisely in the name of freedom. We have also seen in our reflections on Kelsen that relativism contains a dogmatism of its own: this position is so sure of itself that it must be imposed even on those who disagree with it. In the last analysis, there is no way of avoiding here the cynicism that is so obvious in Kelsen and Rorty. If the majority, as in the case of Pilate, is always right, then what truly is right must be trampled upon. For then the only thing that counts is the power of the one who is stronger and knows how to win the majority over to his own views.

The Metaphysical and Christian Thesis

There also exists a position that is strictly antithetical to this skeptical relativism. The father of this other view of political activity is Plato, who assumes that only one who himself knows and has experienced the good is capable of ruling well. All sovereignty must be service, that is, a conscious act whereby one renounces the contemplative height that one has attained and the freedom that this height brings. The act of governing must be a voluntary return into the dark "cave" in which men live. It is only in this way that genuine governance comes about. Anything else is a mere scuffling with illusions in a realm of shadows—and that is in fact what most of political activity is. Plato detects the blindness of average politicians in their fight for power "as if that were a great good".[40] Such reflections bring Plato close to the fundamental biblical idea that truth is not a product of politics. If the relativists genuinely believe that it is, then they are in fact flirting with totalitarianism even though they seek to establish the primacy of freedom, for they make the majority a kind of divinity against which no further appeal is possible.

Such insights led Jacques Maritain to develop a political philosophy that attempts to draw on the great intuitions of the Bible and make these fruitful for political theory. We need not discuss the historical presuppositions of this philosophy here, although that would certainly be worth-while. It suffices to note briefly—at the risk of considerable simplification—that in the modern period the concept of democracy developed along two paths and, hence, on dif-fering foundations. In the Anglo-Saxon sphere, democracy was at least partly conceived and realized on the basis of the tradition of natural law and of a fundamental Christian consensus that certainly had a very pragmatic character.[41] In Rousseau, on the other hand, democracy is employed to attack Christian tradition, and he stands at the head of a stream of thought that tends to conceive of democracy as antithetical to Christianity.[42]

Maritain attempted to dissociate the concept of democ-racy from that of Rousseau and—as he himself said—free it from the Freemasons' dogmas of necessary progress, anthropological optimism, deification of the individual,

[40] *Republic* VU, 520C; see also Possenti, *Le società liberali al bivio*, 290; H. Kuhn, "Plato", in *Klassiker des politischen Denkens*, 3rd ed., ed. H. Maier, H. Rausch, and H. Denzer (Munich, 1969), 1–35.

[41] See Kuhn, *Der Staat*, 263ff.

[42] See R. Spaemann, *Rousseau: Bürger ohne Vaterland* (Munich, 1980).

and forgetfulness of the human person.[43] For him, the primary right of a people to govern itself can never become a right to decide everything. "Government of the people" and "government for the people" belong together, and an equilibrium must be reached between the will of the people and the values that supply the goal of political action. In this sense, Maritain developed a threefold personalism—ontological, axiological, and social—which we cannot discuss in detail here.[44]

It is clear that Christianity is considered here as the source of knowledge, antecedent to the political action on which it sheds light. In order to exclude any suspicion that Christianity might desire a political absolutism, V. Possenti writes, in keeping with Maritain, that the source of truth for politics is not Christianity as revealed religion but Christianity as leaven and a form of life that has proved its worth in the course of history. The truth about the good supplied by the Christian tradition becomes an insight of human reason and hence a rational principle. This truth does not inflict violence on reason or on politics by means of some kind of dogmatism.[45] Naturally, this presupposes a certain amount of optimism about the evidential character of morality and of Christianity, and the relativists would not accept this. This brings us back to the critical point of democratic theory and of its Christian exposition.

Evidential Character of Morality? Mediating Positions

Before we attempt to give an answer, it is helpful to look first at the mediating positions that do not completely fall into one of the two camps. Possenti mentions N. Bobbio,

[43] Possenti, *Le società liberali al bivio*, 309.
[44] See ibid., 308–10.
[45] Ibid., 308ff.

K. Popper, and J. Schumpeter as representatives of such a
middle way; the Cartesian P. Bayle (1647–1706) may be
considered an early forerunner of this position since his
starting point is a strict distinction between metaphysical
and moral truth. In Bayle's view, political life does not
require metaphysics. Metaphysical questions may safely
remain controversial; they are assigned to a pluralist sphere
that is not touched by politics. Practical truth is a sufficient basis for the existence of the community of a state.
Bayle is optimistic about the possibility of discerning this
practical truth. Subsequent generations lost this optimism
long ago, but he could still hold that moral truth is obvious to everyone. There is only one single, universal, and
necessary morality, a true and clear light perceived by all
persons, provided only that they open their eyes. This one
moral truth comes from God, and every individual law
and norm must take this truth as its point of reference.[46]
Bayle is simply describing here the universal consciousness of his own century. The basic moral insights revealed
by Christianity were so obvious to all and so incontrovertible that even in the conflict between confessions they
could be regarded as insights that every rational man took
for granted. They possessed a rational evidential quality
that remained unaffected by the dogmatic disputes of a
divided Christendom.

But what seemed a compelling, God-given insight of
reason retained its evidential character only for as long as
the entire culture, the entire existential context, bore the
imprint of Christian tradition. The moral dimension lost
its evidential quality with the crumbling of the fundamental Christian consensus. All that remained was a naked reason that refused to learn from any historical reality but was

[46] See ibid., 291.

willing to listen only to its own self. Reason, by cutting off its roots in the faith of a historical and religious culture and wishing now to be nothing more than empirical reason, became blind. Where that which is experimentally verifiable became the only accepted shared certainty, the only criterion left to evaluate those truths that went beyond the purely material sphere was their functioning, the interplay between majority and minority. As we have seen, however, this isolation necessarily leads to cynicism and to the destruction of man. The real problem that confronts us today is reason's blindness to the entire nonmaterial dimension of reality.

It will suffice here to look briefly at the social philosophy of K. Popper, who attempts to hang onto Bayle's fundamental vision and salvage it for a relativistic age. Popper's vision of an open society includes free discussion and institutions that guard freedom and protect the disadvantaged. The values on which democracy—as the best form of realizing the open society—is based are recognized by means of a moral faith. They are not to be justified by an appeal to reason. A process of criticism and insight akin to the advancement of science brings us closer to truth. This means that the principles of society cannot be justified or discussed. In the end, one must make a decision about them.[47]

Clearly, many elements contribute to this vision. On the one hand, Popper sees that in the process of free discussion a moral truth possesses no evidential quality. On the other hand, however, he holds that it is possible to grasp this evidential quality in a kind of rational faith. Popper knows perfectly well that the majority principle cannot be permitted to hold sway unconditionally. Bayle's great idea of the shared certainty of reason on moral issues has

[47] Ibid., 301.

shrunk here to a faith that feels its way forward through discussions—and yet, even though the ground on which it stands is shaky, this faith discloses fundamental elements of moral truth and removes them from the realm of pure functionalism. If we look at the whole picture, we may surely say that this slender remnant of rational basic moral certainty is not the product of reason alone but is based on a surviving remnant of insights from the Jewish-Christian tradition. Even this remnant has itself long ceased to be an undisputed certainty. But a minimum of morality is somehow still accessible in the decomposing Christian culture.

Let us look back before we attempt our own answer. We must reject the absolute state that posits itself as the source of truth and law. We must also reject a strict relativism and functionalism, because the elevation of truth to the unique source of law threatens the moral dignity of man and tends toward totalitarianism. This means that the spectrum of acceptable theories would go from Maritain to Popper. Maritain has the greatest confidence in the rational evidential quality of the moral truth of Christianity and of the Christian image of man. Popper exemplifies the least measure of confidence, but this minimum is just enough to ward off a collapse into positivism.

I do not wish to offer a new theory about the relationship between the state and moral truth, either complementing these authors or mediating between them. All I wish is to attempt to summarize the insights that we have encountered so far. They could form a kind of platform that permits a conversation between those political philosophies that in some way or other consider Christianity and its moral message to be a point of reference of political conduct, without thereby blurring the borders between politics and faith.

d. Summary and Conclusions

I believe that we can summarize the conclusions of our examination of the modern debate in the following seven statements:

1. The state is not itself the source of truth and morality. It cannot produce truth from its own self by means of an ideology based on people or race or class or some other entity. Nor can it produce truth via the majority. The state is not absolute.

2. The goal of the state cannot consist in a freedom without defined contents. In order to establish a meaningful and viable ordering of life in society, the state requires a minimum of truth, of knowledge of the good, that cannot be manipulated. Otherwise, as Augustine says, it will sink to the level of a smoothly functioning band of robbers, because, like such a band, its definition would be purely functional. It would not be defined on the basis of that justice which is good for everyone.

3. Accordingly, the state must receive from outside itself the essential measure of knowledge and truth with regard to that which is good.

4. This "outside" might, in the best possible scenario, be the pure insight of reason. It would be the task of an independent philosophy to cultivate this insight and keep watch over it. In practice, however, such a pure rational evidential quality independent of history does not exist. Metaphysical and moral reason comes into action only in a historical context. At one and the same time, it depends on this context and transcends it. In fact, all states have recognized and applied moral reason on the basis of antecedent

religious traditions, which also provided moral education. Naturally, openness to reason and the measure of knowledge of the good differs greatly in the historical religions, just as the relationship between state and religion has taken different forms. We find throughout history the temptation to identify the state with divinity and to absolutize it in religious terms. But we certainly also find positive models of a relationship between moral knowledge based on religion and the good ordering of the state.

Indeed, one may say that the great institutions of religion and the state display a fundamental consensus about important elements of what is morally good and that this consensus points to a shared rationality.

5. Christian faith has proved to be the most universal and rational religious culture. Even today, it offers reason the basic structure of moral insight that, if it does not actually lead to some kind of evidential quality, at least furnishes the basis of a rational moral faith without which no society can endure.

6. Accordingly, as I have already observed, the state receives its basic support from outside: not from a mere reason that is inadequate in the moral realm, but from a reason that has come to maturity in the historical form of faith. This distinction must not be canceled out: the Church may not exalt herself to become a state, nor may she seek to work as an organ of power in the state or beyond the state boundaries, for then she would make herself precisely that absolute state that she is meant to rule out. By merging with the state, the Church would destroy both the essence of the state and her own essence.

7. The Church remains something "outside" the state, for only thus can both Church and state be what they are

meant to be. Like the state, the Church too must remain in her own proper place and within her boundaries. She must respect her own being and her own freedom, precisely in order to be able to perform for the state the service that the latter requires. The Church must exert herself with all her vigor so that in her there may shine forth the moral truth that she offers to the state and that ought to become evident to the citizens of the state. This truth must be vigorous within the Church, and it must form men, for only then it will have the power to convince others and to be a force working like a leaven for all of society.[48]

e. Closing Reflection: Heaven and Earth

This gives a new importance to a Christian doctrine of which little was heard in the twentieth century. It is expressed in Paul's words: "Our commonwealth is in heaven" (Phil 3:20).[49] The New Testament affirms this conviction with great emphasis. It understands the city in heaven, not merely as an ideal reality, but as a completely real affair. The new homeland toward which we are journeying is the interior criterion that governs our life and the hope that sustains us in the present day. The New Testament writers know that this city already exists and that we already belong to it, even if we are still en route. The Letter to the Hebrews expresses this idea with particular urgency: "Here we have no lasting city, but we seek the city which is to come" (13:14). The author writes about the presence of this city, which is an effective reality even now: "You have come to Mount Zion and to the city of

---

[48] Soloviev's reflections on Church and state, which deserve to be pondered anew, go in the same direction, although the idea of "theocracy" is not tenable in the form in which he elaborated it. See *La grande controverse et la politique chrétienne* (Paris, 1953), 129–68.

[49] On what follows, see Schlier, *Die Zeit der Kirche*, 7ff.

the living God, the heavenly Jerusalem" (12:22). Accordingly, we may say of Christians what was once said of the patriarchs of Israel: they are foreigners and resident aliens, since their whole efforts tend toward their future fatherland (11:13–16).

For a long time now, Christians have tended to avoid quoting these texts, since they appear to alienate man from the earth and prevent him from fulfilling his innerworldly task, which is also a political task. Nietzsche called out, over a hundred years ago: "Brothers, remain faithful to the earth!" And the mighty Marxist tendency that was hammered into us held that time devoted to heaven is time wasted. Bertold Brecht said we should leave heaven to the sparrows,[50] while we ourselves take care of the earth and make it a place where we can live.

In reality, it is precisely this "eschatological" attitude that guarantees the state its own rights while simultaneously resisting absolutism by indicating the boundaries both of the state and of the Church in the world. Where this fundamental attitude prevails, the Church knows that she cannot be a state here on earth, for she is aware that the definitive state lies elsewhere, and that she cannot set up the city of God on earth. She respects the earthly state as an institution belonging to historical time, with rights and laws that the Church recognizes. This is why she demands loyalty and collaboration with the earthly state, even when this is not a Christian state (Rom 13:1; 1 Pet 2:13–17; 1 Tim 2:2). By demanding both loyal cooperation with the state and respect for its specific nature and its limitations, the Church provides an education in those virtues that allow a state to become good. At the same time, she puts

---

[50] There is a play on words in German: *Himmel* means both "heaven" and "sky". —TRANS.

up a barrier against the omnipotence of the state. Because one "must obey God rather than men" (Acts 5:29), and because the Church has learned from the Word of God what is good and what is evil, she sounds the cry for resistance wherever the state might demand something genuinely evil and opposed to God.

The fact that Christians are journeying toward the other city does not alienate them. In reality, it is this that allows us to be healthy and our states to be healthy. For if men have nothing more to expect than what this world offers them, and if they may and must demand all this from the state, they destroy both their own selves and every human society. If we do not want to get entangled anew in the tentacles of totalitarianism, we must look beyond the state, which is only one part, not the totality.

There is no antithesis between hope for heaven and loyalty to the earth, since this hope is also hope for the earth. While we hope for something greater and definitive, we Christians may and must bring hope into that which is transitory, into the world of our states.

VII

The Ethical Foundations
of Political Choices

The Speech in Westminster Hall
(September 17, 2010)

Mr. Speaker,

Thank you for your words of welcome on behalf of this distinguished gathering. As I address you, I am conscious of the privilege afforded me to speak to the British people and their representatives in Westminster Hall, a building of unique significance in the civil and political history of the people of these islands. Allow me also to express my esteem for the Parliament which has existed on this site for centuries and which has had such a profound influence on the development of participative government among the

On the late afternoon of September 17, 2010, while on his apostolic visit to the United Kingdom, the Holy Father, Benedict XVI, traveled to Westminster Hall in London to meet with representatives of British society including the diplomatic corps, politicians, academics, and business leaders. Upon his arrival, the Holy Father was greeted by the Speaker of the House of Lords and the House of Commons and introduced by Yeoman Usher of the Black Rod. Then, after greeting the Hon. John Bercow, Speaker of the House of Commons, the Holy Father gave the following address. Translation from the Vatican website.

nations, especially in the Commonwealth and the English-speaking world at large. Your common law tradition serves as the basis of legal systems in many parts of the world, and your particular vision of the respective rights and duties of the state and the individual, and of the separation of powers, remains an inspiration to many across the globe.

As I speak to you in this historic setting, I think of the countless men and women down the centuries who have played their part in the momentous events that have taken place within these walls and have shaped the lives of many generations of Britons, and others besides. In particular, I recall the figure of Saint Thomas More, the great English scholar and statesman, who is admired by believers and nonbelievers alike for the integrity with which he followed his conscience, even at the cost of displeasing the sovereign whose "good servant" he was, because he chose to serve God first. The dilemma which faced More in those difficult times, the perennial question of the relationship between what is owed to Caesar and what is owed to God, allows me the opportunity to reflect with you briefly on the proper place of religious belief within the political process.

This country's Parliamentary tradition owes much to the national instinct for moderation, to the desire to achieve a genuine balance between the legitimate claims of government and the rights of those subject to it. While decisive steps have been taken at several points in your history to place limits on the exercise of power, the nation's political institutions have been able to evolve with a remarkable degree of stability. In the process, Britain has emerged as a pluralist democracy which places great value on freedom of speech, freedom of political affiliation and respect for the rule of law, with a strong sense of the individual's rights and duties, and of the equality of all citizens before the law. While couched in different language, Catholic social teaching has much in common with this approach, in its overriding concern to safeguard the unique dignity of every human person, created in the image and likeness of God, and in its emphasis on the duty of civil authority to foster the common good.

And yet the fundamental questions at stake in Thomas More's trial continue to present themselves in ever-changing terms as new social conditions emerge. Each generation, as it seeks to advance the common good, must ask anew: What are the requirements that governments may reasonably impose upon citizens, and how far do they extend? By appeal to what authority can moral dilemmas be resolved? These questions take us directly to the ethical foundations of civil discourse. If the moral principles underpinning the democratic process are themselves determined by nothing more solid than social consensus, then the fragility of the process becomes all too evident—herein lies the real challenge for democracy.

The inadequacy of pragmatic, short-term solutions to complex social and ethical problems has been illustrated all too clearly by the recent global financial crisis. There is widespread agreement that the lack of a solid ethical foundation for economic activity has contributed to the grave difficulties now being experienced by millions of people throughout the world. Just as "every economic decision has a moral consequence" (*Caritas in Veritate*, 37), so too in the political field, the ethical dimension of policy has far-reaching consequences that no government can afford to ignore. A positive illustration of this is found in one of the British Parliament's particularly notable achievements— the abolition of the slave trade. The campaign that led to this landmark legislation was built upon firm ethical principles, rooted in the natural law, and it has made a contribution to civilization of which this nation may be justly proud.

The central question at issue, then, is this: Where is the ethical foundation for political choices to be found? The Catholic tradition maintains that the objective norms governing right action are accessible to reason, prescinding from the content of revelation. According to this understanding, the role of religion in political debate is not so much to supply these norms, as if they could not be known by nonbelievers—still less to propose concrete political solutions, which would lie altogether outside the competence of religion—but rather to help purify and shed light upon the application of reason to the discovery of objective moral principles. This "corrective" role of religion vis-à-vis reason is not always welcomed, though, partly because distorted forms of religion, such as sectarianism and fundamentalism, can be seen to create serious social problems themselves. And in their turn, these distortions of religion arise when insufficient attention is given to the purifying and structuring role of reason within religion. It is a two-way process. Without the corrective supplied by religion, though, reason too can fall prey to distortions, as when it is manipulated by ideology or applied in a partial way that fails to take full account of the dignity of the human person. Such misuse of reason, after all, was what gave rise to the slave trade in the first place and to many other social evils, not least the totalitarian ideologies of the twentieth century. This is why I would suggest that the world of reason and the world of faith—the world of secular rationality and the world of religious belief—need one another and should not be afraid to enter into a profound and ongoing dialogue, for the good of our civilization.

Religion, in other words, is not a problem for legislators to solve, but a vital contributor to the national conversation. In this light, I cannot but voice my concern at the increasing marginalization of religion, particularly of Christianity, that is taking place in some quarters, even in nations which place a great emphasis on tolerance. There are those who would advocate that the voice of religion be silenced, or at least relegated to the purely private sphere. There are those who argue that the public celebration of festivals such as Christmas should be discouraged, in the questionable belief that it might somehow offend those of other religions or none. And there are those who argue—paradoxically with the intention of eliminating discrimination—that Christians in public roles should be required at times to act against their conscience. These are worrying signs of a failure to appreciate not only the rights of believers to freedom of conscience and freedom of religion, but also the legitimate role of religion in the public square. I would invite all of you, therefore, within your respective spheres of influence, to seek ways of promoting and encouraging dialogue between faith and reason at every level of national life.

Your readiness to do so is already implied in the unprecedented invitation extended to me today. And it finds expression in the fields of concern in which your Government has been engaged with the Holy See. In the area of peace, there have been exchanges regarding the elaboration of an international arms trade treaty; regarding human rights, the Holy See and the United Kingdom have welcomed the spread of democracy, especially in the last sixty-five years; in the field of development, there has been collaboration on debt relief, fair trade and financing for development, particularly through the International Finance Facility, the International Immunization Bond, and the Advanced Market Commitment. The Holy See also looks forward to exploring with the United Kingdom new ways to promote environmental responsibility, to the benefit of all.

I also note that the present Government has committed the United Kingdom to devoting 0.7% of national income to development aid by 2013. In recent years it has been encouraging to witness the positive signs of a worldwide growth in solidarity toward the poor. But to turn this solidarity into effective action calls for fresh thinking that will improve life conditions in many important areas, such as food production, clean water, job creation, education, support to families, especially migrants, and basic healthcare. Where human lives are concerned, time is always short: yet the world has witnessed the vast resources that governments can draw upon to rescue financial institutions deemed "too big to fail". Surely the integral human development of the world's peoples is no less important: here is an enterprise, worthy of the world's attention, that is truly "too big to fail".

This overview of recent cooperation between the United Kingdom and the Holy See illustrates well how much progress has been made, in the years that have passed since the establishment of bilateral diplomatic relations, in promoting throughout the world the many core values that we share. I hope and pray that this relationship will continue to bear fruit and that it will be mirrored in a growing acceptance of the need for dialogue and respect at every level of society between the world of reason and the world of faith. I am convinced that, within this country, too, there are many areas in which the Church and the public authorities can work together for the good of citizens, in harmony with Britain's long-standing tradition. For such cooperation to be possible, religious bodies—including institutions linked to the Catholic Church—need to be free to act in accordance with their own principles and specific convictions based upon the faith and the official teaching of the Church. In this way, such basic rights as religious freedom, freedom of conscience, and freedom of association are guaranteed. The angels looking down on us from the magnificent ceiling of this ancient Hall remind us of the long tradition from which British Parliamentary democracy has evolved. They remind us that God is constantly watching over us to guide and protect us. And they summon us to acknowledge the vital contribution that religious belief has made and can continue to make to the life of the nation.

Mr. Speaker, I thank you once again for this opportunity briefly to address this distinguished audience. Let me assure you and the Lord Speaker of my continued good wishes and prayers for you and for the fruitful work of both Houses of this ancient Parliament. Thank you and God bless you all!

VIII

Affirming the Right to
Combat Injustice

The Speech to the Bundestag
(September 22, 2011)

Mr. President of the Federal Republic,
Mr. President of the Bundestag,
Madam Chancellor,
Madam President of the Bundesrat,
Ladies and Gentlemen Members of the House,

It is an honor and a joy for me to speak before this distinguished house, before the Parliament of my native Germany, that meets here as a democratically elected representation of the people, in order to work for the good of the Federal Republic of Germany. I should like to thank the President of the *Bundestag* both for his invitation to deliver this address and for the kind words of greeting and appreciation with which he has welcomed me. At this moment I turn to you, distinguished ladies and gentlemen, not least as your fellow-countryman who for all his life

Pope Benedict XVI, "The Listening Heart: Reflections on the Foundations of Law", Address to the Bundestag, September 22, 2011. Translation from the Vatican website.

has been conscious of close links to his origins and has followed the affairs of his native Germany with keen interest. But the invitation to give this address was extended to me as Pope, as the Bishop of Rome, who bears the highest responsibility for Catholic Christianity. In issuing this invitation you are acknowledging the role that the Holy See plays as a partner within the community of peoples and states. Setting out from this international responsibility that I hold, I should like to propose to you some thoughts on the foundations of a free state of law.

Allow me to begin my reflections on the foundations of law [*Recht*] with a brief story from sacred Scripture. In the First Book of the Kings, it is recounted that God invited the young King Solomon, on his accession to the throne, to make a request. What will the young ruler ask for at this important moment? Success—wealth—long life—destruction of his enemies? He chooses none of these things. Instead, he asks for a listening heart so that he may govern God's people and discern between good and evil (cf. 1 Kg 3:9). Through this story, the Bible wants to tell us what should ultimately matter for a politician. His fundamental criterion and the motivation for his work as a politician must not be success, and certainly not material gain. Politics must be a striving for justice, and hence it has to establish the fundamental preconditions for peace. Naturally a politician will seek success, without which he would have no opportunity for effective political action at all. Yet success is subordinated to the criterion of justice, to the will to do what is right, and to the understanding of what is right. Success can also be seductive and thus can open up the path toward the falsification of what is right, toward the destruction of justice. "Without justice—what else is the state but a great band of robbers?", as Saint Augustine once said. We Germans know from our own experience that these words are no empty specter. We have seen how power became divorced from right, how power opposed right and crushed it, so that the state became an instrument for destroying right—a highly organized band of robbers, capable of threatening the whole world and driving it to the edge of the abyss. To serve right and to fight against the dominion of wrong is and remains the fundamental task of the politician. At a moment in history when man has acquired previously inconceivable power, this task takes on a particular urgency. Man can destroy the world. He can manipulate himself. He can, so to speak, make human beings and he can deny them their humanity. How do we recognize what is right? How can we discern between good and evil, between what is truly right and what may appear right? Even now, Solomon's request remains the decisive issue facing politicians and politics today.

For most of the matters that need to be regulated by law, the support of the majority can serve as a sufficient criterion. Yet it is evident that for the fundamental issues of law, in which the dignity of man and of humanity is at stake, the majority principle is not enough: everyone in a position of responsibility must personally seek out the criteria to be followed when framing laws. In the third century, the great theologian Origen provided the following explanation for the resistance of Christians to certain legal systems: "Suppose that a man were living among the Scythians, whose laws are contrary to the divine law, and was compelled to live among them ... such a man for the sake of the true law, though illegal among the Scythians, would rightly form associations with like-minded people contrary to the laws of the Scythians."[1]

---

[1] *Contra Celsum*, bk. 1, chap. 1. Cf. A. Fürst, "Monotheismus und Monarchie. Zum Zusammenhang von Heil und Herrschaft in der Antike", *Theol. Phil.* 81 (2006): 321–38, quoted on p. 336; cf. also J. Ratzinger, *Die Einheit der Nationen. Eine Vision der Kirchenväter* (Salzburg and Munich, 1971), 60.

This conviction was what motivated resistance movements to act against the Nazi regime and other totalitarian
regimes, thereby doing a great service to justice and to
humanity as a whole. For these people, it was indisputably
evident that the law in force was actually unlawful. Yet
when it comes to the decisions of a democratic politician,
the question of what now corresponds to the law of truth,
what is actually right and may be enacted as law, is less
obvious. In terms of the underlying anthropological issues,
what is right and may be given the force of law is in no
way simply self-evident today. The question of how to
recognize what is truly right and thus to serve justice when
framing laws has never been simple, and today in view of
the vast extent of our knowledge and our capacity, it has
become still harder.

How do we recognize what is right? In history, systems
of law have almost always been based on religion: decisions regarding what was to be lawful among men were
taken with reference to the divinity. Unlike other great
religions, Christianity has never proposed a revealed law
to the state and to society, that is to say, a juridical order
derived from revelation. Instead, it has pointed to nature
and reason as the true sources of law—and to the harmony
of objective and subjective reason, which naturally presupposes that both spheres are rooted in the creative reason
of God. Christian theologians thereby aligned themselves
with a philosophical and juridical movement that began
to take shape in the second century B.C. In the first half
of that century, the social natural law developed by the
Stoic philosophers came into contact with leading teachers of Roman law.[2] Through this encounter, the juridical

---

[2] Cf. W. Waldstein, *Ins Herz geschrieben: Das Naturrecht als Fundament einer menschlichen Gesellschaft* (Augsburg, 2010), pp. 11ff., 31–61.

culture of the West was born, which was and is of key significance for the juridical culture of mankind. This pre-Christian marriage between law and philosophy opened up the path that led via the Christian Middle Ages and the juridical developments of the Age of Enlightenment all the way to the Declaration of Human Rights and to our German Basic Law of 1949, with which our nation committed itself to "inviolable and inalienable human rights as the foundation of every human community, and of peace and justice in the world".

For the development of law and for the development of humanity, it was highly significant that Christian theologians aligned themselves against the religious law associated with polytheism and on the side of philosophy and that they acknowledged reason and nature in their interrelation as the universally valid source of law. This step had already been taken by Saint Paul in the Letter to the Romans, when he said: "When Gentiles who have not the Law [the Torah of Israel] do by nature what the law requires, they are a law to themselves ... they show that what the law requires is written on their hearts, while their conscience also bears witness ..." (Rom 2:14f.). Here we see the two fundamental concepts of nature and conscience, where conscience is nothing other than Solomon's listening heart, reason that is open to the language of being. If this seemed to offer a clear explanation of the foundations of legislation up to the time of the Enlightenment, up to the time of the Declaration of Human Rights after the Second World War and the framing of our Basic Law, there has been a dramatic shift in the situation in the last half-century. The idea of natural law is today viewed as a specifically Catholic doctrine, not worth bringing into the discussion in a non-Catholic environment, so that one feels almost ashamed even to mention the term. Let me outline briefly how this situation arose. Fundamentally it is because of the idea that an unbridgeable gulf exists between "is" and "ought". An "ought" can never follow from an "is", because the two are situated on completely different planes. The reason for this is that in the meantime, the positivist understanding of nature has come to be almost universally accepted. If nature—in the words of Hans Kelsen—is viewed as "an aggregate of objective data linked together in terms of cause and effect", then indeed no ethical indication of any kind can be derived from it.[3] A positivist conception of nature as purely functional, as the natural sciences consider it to be, is incapable of producing any bridge to ethics and law, but once again yields only functional answers. The same also applies to reason, according to the positivist understanding that is widely held to be the only genuinely scientific one. Anything that is not verifiable or falsifiable, according to this understanding, does not belong to the realm of reason strictly understood. Hence ethics and religion must be assigned to the subjective field, and they remain extraneous to the realm of reason in the strict sense of the word. Where positivist reason dominates the field to the exclusion of all else— and that is broadly the case in our public mind-set—then the classical sources of knowledge for ethics and law are excluded. This is a dramatic situation which affects everyone, and on which a public debate is necessary. Indeed, an essential goal of this address is to issue an urgent invitation to launch one.

The positivist approach to nature and reason, the positivist world view in general, is a most important dimension of human knowledge and capacity that we may in no way dispense with. But in and of itself it is not a sufficient

[3] Ibid., 15–21.

culture corresponding to the full breadth of the human condition. Where positivist reason considers itself the only sufficient culture and banishes all other cultural realities to the status of subcultures, it diminishes man, indeed it threatens his humanity. I say this with Europe specifically in mind, where there are concerted efforts to recognize only positivism as a common culture and a common basis for law-making, reducing all the other insights and values of our culture to the level of subculture, with the result that Europe vis-à-vis other world cultures is left in a state of culturelessness and at the same time extremist and radical movements emerge to fill the vacuum. In its self-proclaimed exclusivity, the positivist reason which recognizes nothing beyond mere functionality resembles a concrete bunker with no windows, in which we ourselves provide lighting and atmospheric conditions, being no longer willing to obtain either from God's wide world. And yet we cannot hide from ourselves the fact that even in this artificial world, we are still covertly drawing upon God's raw materials, which we refashion into our own products. The windows must be flung open again, we must see the wide world, the sky and the earth, once more and learn to make proper use of all this.

But how are we to do this? How do we find our way out into the wide world, into the big picture? How can reason rediscover its true greatness without being sidetracked into irrationality? How can nature reassert itself in its true depth, with all its demands, with all its directives? I would like to recall one of the developments in recent political history, hoping that I will neither be misunderstood nor provoke too many one-sided polemics. I would say that the emergence of the ecological movement in German politics since the 1970s, while it has not exactly flung open the windows, nevertheless was and continues to be a cry for fresh air which must not be ignored or pushed aside, just because too much of it is seen to be irrational. Young people had come to realize that something is wrong in our relationship with nature, that matter is not just raw material for us to shape at will, but that the earth has a dignity of its own and that we must follow its directives. In saying this, I am clearly not promoting any particular political party—nothing could be further from my mind. If something is wrong in our relationship with reality, then we must all reflect seriously on the whole situation and we are all prompted to question the very foundations of our culture. Allow me to dwell a little longer on this point. The importance of ecology is no longer disputed. We must listen to the language of nature, and we must answer accordingly. Yet I would like to underline a point that seems to me to be neglected, today as in the past: there is also an ecology of man. Man too has a nature that he must respect and that he cannot manipulate at will. Man is not merely self-creating freedom. Man does not create himself. He is intellect and will, but he is also nature, and his will is rightly ordered if he respects his nature, listens to it, and accepts himself for who he is, as one who did not create himself. In this way, and in no other, is true human freedom fulfilled.

Let us come back to the fundamental concepts of nature and reason from which we set out. The great proponent of legal positivism, Kelsen, at the age of 84—in 1965—abandoned the dualism of "is" and "ought". (I find it comforting that rational thought is evidently still possible at the age of 84!) Previously he had said that norms can only come from the will. Nature therefore could only contain norms, he adds, if a will had put them there. But this, he says, would presuppose a Creator God, whose will had entered into nature. "Any attempt to discuss the truth of this belief is utterly futile", he observed.[4] Is it really?—I find myself asking. Is it really pointless to wonder whether the objective reason that manifests itself in nature does not presuppose a creative reason, a *Creator Spiritus*?

At this point Europe's cultural heritage ought to come to our assistance. The conviction that there is a Creator God is what gave rise to the idea of human rights, the idea of the equality of all people before the law, the recognition of the inviolability of human dignity in every single person, and the awareness of people's responsibility for their actions. Our cultural memory is shaped by these rational insights. To ignore it or dismiss it as a thing of the past would be to dismember our culture totally and to rob it of its completeness. The culture of Europe arose from the encounter between Jerusalem, Athens, and Rome— from the encounter between Israel's monotheism, the philosophical reason of the Greeks and Roman law. This three-way encounter has shaped the inner identity of Europe. In the awareness of man's responsibility before God and in the acknowledgment of the inviolable dignity of every single human person, it has established criteria of law: it is these criteria that we are called to defend at this moment in our history.

As he assumed the mantle of office, the young King Solomon was invited to make a request. How would it be if we, the law-makers of today, were invited to make a request? What would we ask for? I think that, even today, there is ultimately nothing else we could wish for but a listening heart—the capacity to discern between good and evil, and thus to establish true law, to serve justice and peace. I thank you for your attention!

[4] Cf. Ibid., 19.

IX

Blessed Are the Peacemakers

Message for the 46th World Day of Peace (January 1, 2013)

1. Each new year brings the expectation of a better world. In light of this, I ask God, the Father of humanity, to grant us concord and peace, so that the aspirations of all for a happy and prosperous life may be achieved.

Fifty years after the beginning of the Second Vatican Council, which helped to strengthen the Church's mission in the world, it is heartening to realize that Christians, as the People of God in fellowship with him and sojourning among mankind, are committed within history to sharing humanity's joys and hopes, grief and anguish,[1] as they proclaim the salvation of Christ and promote peace for all.

In effect, our times, marked by globalization with its positive and negative aspects, as well as the continuation of violent conflicts and threats of war, demand a new, shared

Pope Benedict XVI, World Day of Peace Message, 2013. Translation from the Vatican website.

[1] Cf. Second Vatican Ecumenical Council, Pastoral Constitution on the Church in the Modern World, *Gaudium et Spes*, 1.

commitment in pursuit of the common good and the development of all men, and of the whole man.

It is alarming to see hotbeds of tension and conflict caused by growing instances of inequality between rich and poor, by the prevalence of a selfish and individualistic mind-set which also finds expression in an unregulated financial capitalism. In addition to the varied forms of terrorism and international crime, peace is also endangered by those forms of fundamentalism and fanaticism which distort the true nature of religion, which is called to foster fellowship and reconciliation among people.

All the same, the many different efforts at peacemaking which abound in our world testify to mankind's innate vocation to peace. In every person the desire for peace is an essential aspiration which coincides in a certain way with the desire for a full, happy, and successful human life. In other words, the desire for peace corresponds to a fundamental moral principle, namely, the duty and right to an integral social and communitarian development, which is part of God's plan for mankind. Man is made for the peace which is God's gift.

All of this led me to draw inspiration for this Message from the words of Jesus Christ: "Blessed are the peacemakers, for they will be called children of God" (Mt 5:9).

Gospel Beatitude

2. The beatitudes which Jesus proclaimed (cf. Mt 5:3–12 and Lk 6:20–23) are promises. In the biblical tradition, the beatitude is a literary genre which always involves some good news, a "gospel", which culminates in a promise. Therefore, the beatitudes are not only moral exhortations whose observance foresees in due time—ordinarily in the next life—a reward or a situation of future happiness.

Rather, the blessedness of which the beatitudes speak
consists in the fulfillment of a promise made to all those
who allow themselves to be guided by the requirements
of truth, justice, and love. In the eyes of the world, those
who trust in God and his promises often appear naïve or far
from reality. Yet Jesus tells them that not only in the next
life, but already in this life, they will discover that they are
children of God, and that God has always been, and ever
will be, completely on their side. They will understand
that they are not alone, because he is on the side of those
committed to truth, justice, and love. Jesus, the revelation
of the Father's love, does not hesitate to offer himself in
self-sacrifice. Once we accept Jesus Christ, God and man,
we have the joyful experience of an immense gift: the
sharing of God's own life, the life of grace, the pledge of
a fully blessed existence. Jesus Christ, in particular, grants
us true peace, which is born of the trusting encounter of
man with God.

Jesus' beatitude tells us that peace is both a messianic
gift and the fruit of human effort. In effect, peace presupposes a humanism open to transcendence. It is the fruit
of the reciprocal gift, of a mutual enrichment, thanks to
the gift which has its source in God and enables us to live
with others and for others. The ethics of peace is an ethics
of fellowship and sharing. It is indispensable, then, that
the various cultures in our day overcome forms of anthropology and ethics based on technical and practical suppo-
sitions which are merely subjectivistic and pragmatic, in
virtue of which relationships of coexistence are inspired by
criteria of power or profit, means become ends and vice
versa, and culture and education are centered on instruments, technique, and efficiency alone. The precondition
for peace is the dismantling of the dictatorship of relativism and of the supposition of a completely autonomous

morality which precludes acknowledgment of the ineluc-
table natural moral law inscribed by God upon the conscience of every man and woman. Peace is the building
up of coexistence in rational and moral terms, based on
a foundation whose measure is not created by man, but
rather by God. As Psalm 29 puts it: "May the Lord give
strength to his people; may the Lord bless his people with
peace" (v. 11).

Peace: God's Gift and the Fruit of Human Effort

3. Peace concerns the human person as a whole, and it
involves complete commitment. It is peace with God
through a life lived according to his will. It is interior
peace with oneself, and exterior peace with our neighbors
and all creation. Above all, as Blessed John XXIII wrote
in his Encyclical *Pacem in Terris*, whose fiftieth anniversary
will fall in a few months, it entails the building up of a
coexistence based on truth, freedom, love, and justice.[2]
The denial of what makes up the true nature of human
beings in its essential dimensions, its intrinsic capacity to
know the true and the good and, ultimately, to know
God himself, jeopardizes peacemaking. Without the truth
about man inscribed by the Creator in the human heart,
freedom and love become debased and justice loses the
ground of its exercise.

To become authentic peacemakers, it is fundamental to
keep in mind our transcendent dimension and to enter
into constant dialogue with God, the Father of mercy,
whereby we implore the redemption achieved for us by
his only-begotten Son. In this way mankind can overcome
that progressive dimming and rejection of peace which is

[2] Cf. Encyclical Letter *Pacem in Terris* (April 11, 1963): *AAS* 55 (1963),
265–66.

sin in all its forms: selfishness and violence, greed and the will to power and dominion, intolerance, hatred, and unjust structures.

The attainment of peace depends above all on recognizing that we are, in God, one human family. This family is structured, as the Encyclical *Pacem in Terris* taught, by interpersonal relations and institutions supported and animated by a communitarian "we", which entails an internal and external moral order in which, in accordance with truth and justice, reciprocal rights and mutual duties are sincerely recognized. Peace is an order enlivened and integrated by love, in such a way that we feel the needs of others as our own, share our goods with others, and work throughout the world for greater communion in spiritual values. It is an order achieved in freedom, that is, in a way consistent with the dignity of persons who, by their very nature as rational beings, take responsibility for their own actions.[3]

Peace is not a dream or something utopian; it is possible. Our gaze needs to go deeper, beneath superficial appearances and phenomena, to discern a positive reality which exists in human hearts, since every man and woman has been created in the image of God and is called to grow and contribute to the building of a new world. God himself, through the incarnation of his Son and his work of redemption, has entered into history and has brought about a new creation and a new covenant between God and man (cf. Jer 31:31–34), thus enabling us to have a "new heart" and a "new spirit" (cf. Ez 36:26).

For this very reason the Church is convinced of the urgency of a new proclamation of Jesus Christ, the first and fundamental factor of the integral development of

[3] Cf. ibid.: *AAS* 55 (1963), 266.

peoples and also of peace. Jesus is indeed our peace, our justice, and our reconciliation (cf. Eph 2:14; 2 Cor 5:18). The peacemaker, according to Jesus' beatitude, is the one who seeks the good of the other, the fullness of good in body and soul, today and tomorrow.

From this teaching one can infer that each person and every community, whether religious, civil, educational, or cultural, is called to work for peace. Peace is principally the attainment of the common good in society at its different levels, primary and intermediary, national, international, and global. Precisely for this reason it can be said that the paths which lead to the attainment of the common good are also the paths that must be followed in the pursuit of peace.

Peacemakers Are Those Who Love, Defend, and Promote Life in Its Fullness

4. The path to the attainment of the common good and to peace is above all that of respect for human life in all its many aspects, beginning with its conception, through its development, and up to its natural end. True peacemakers, then, are those who love, defend, and promote human life in all its dimensions, personal, communitarian, and transcendent. Life in its fullness is the height of peace. Anyone who loves peace cannot tolerate attacks and crimes against life.

Those who insufficiently value human life and, in consequence, support among other things the liberalization of abortion perhaps do not realize that in this way they are proposing the pursuit of a false peace. The flight from responsibility, which degrades human persons, and even more so the killing of a defenseless and innocent being, will never be able to produce happiness or peace. Indeed how could one claim to bring about peace, the integral development of peoples, or even the protection of the environment without defending the life of those who are weakest, beginning with the unborn. Every offense against life, especially at its beginning, inevitably causes irreparable damage to development, peace, and the environment. Neither is it just to introduce surreptitiously into legislation false rights or freedoms which, on the basis of a reductive and relativistic view of human beings and the clever use of ambiguous expressions aimed at promoting a supposed right to abortion and euthanasia, pose a threat to the fundamental right to life.

There is also a need to acknowledge and promote the natural structure of marriage as the union of a man and a woman in the face of attempts to make it juridically equivalent to radically different types of union; such attempts actually harm and help to destabilize marriage, obscuring its specific nature and its indispensable role in society.

These principles are not truths of faith, nor are they simply a corollary of the right to religious freedom. They are inscribed in human nature itself, accessible to reason, and thus common to all humanity. The Church's efforts to promote them are not therefore confessional in character, but addressed to all people, whatever their religious affiliation. Efforts of this kind are all the more necessary the more these principles are denied or misunderstood, since this constitutes an offense against the truth of the human person, with serious harm to justice and peace.

Consequently, another important way of helping to build peace is for legal systems and the administration of justice to recognize the right to invoke the principle of conscientious objection in the face of laws or government measures that offend against human dignity, such as abortion and euthanasia.

One of the fundamental human rights, also with reference to international peace, is the right of individuals and communities to religious freedom. At this stage in history, it is becoming increasingly important to promote this right not only from the negative point of view, as *freedom from*—for example, obligations or limitations involving the freedom to choose one's religion—but also from the positive point of view, in its various expressions, as *freedom for*—for example, bearing witness to one's religion, making its teachings known, engaging in activities in the educational, benevolent, and charitable fields which permit the practice of religious precepts, and existing and acting as social bodies structured in accordance with the proper doctrinal principles and institutional ends of each. Sadly, even in countries of long-standing Christian tradition, instances of religious intolerance are becoming more numerous, especially in relation to Christianity and those who simply wear identifying signs of their religion.

Peacemakers must also bear in mind that, in growing sectors of public opinion, the ideologies of radical liberalism and technocracy are spreading the conviction that economic growth should be pursued even to the detriment of the state's social responsibilities and civil society's networks of solidarity, together with social rights and duties. It should be remembered that these rights and duties are fundamental for the full realization of other rights and duties, starting with those which are civil and political.

One of the social rights and duties most under threat today is the right to work. The reason for this is that labor and the rightful recognition of workers' juridical status are increasingly undervalued, since economic development is thought to depend principally on completely free markets. Labor is thus regarded as a variable dependent on economic and financial mechanisms. In this regard, I would reaffirm that human dignity and economic, social, and political factors demand that we continue "to prioritize the goal of access to steady employment for everyone".[4] If this ambitious goal is to be realized, one prior condition is a fresh outlook on work, based on ethical principles and spiritual values that reinforce the notion of work as a fundamental good for the individual, for the family, and for society. Corresponding to this good are a duty and a right that demand courageous new policies of universal employment.

Building the Good of Peace through a New Model of Development and Economics

5. In many quarters it is now recognized that a new model of development is needed, as well as a new approach to the economy. Both integral, sustainable development in solidarity and the common good require a correct scale of goods and values which can be structured with God as the ultimate point of reference. It is not enough to have many different means and choices at one's disposal, however good these may be. Both the wide variety of goods fostering development and the presence of a wide range of choices must be employed against the horizon of a good life, an upright conduct that acknowledges the primacy of the spiritual and the call to work for the common good. Otherwise they lose their real value and end up becoming new idols.

In order to emerge from the present financial and economic crisis—which has engendered ever greater inequalities—we need people, groups, and institutions which will promote life by fostering human creativity, in order to draw from the crisis itself an opportunity for discernment and for a new economic model. The

---

[4] Benedict XVI, Encyclical Letter *Caritas in Veritate* (June 29, 2009), 32: *AAS* 101 (2009), 666–67.

predominant model of recent decades called for seeking
maximum profit and consumption, on the basis of an individualistic and selfish mind-set, aimed at considering individuals solely in terms of their ability to meet the demands
of competitiveness. Yet, from another standpoint, true and
lasting success is attained through the gift of ourselves, our
intellectual abilities, and our entrepreneurial skills, since a
"livable" or truly human economic development requires
the principle of gratuitousness as an expression of fraternity and the logic of gift.[5] Concretely, in economic activity, peacemakers are those who establish bonds of fairness
and reciprocity with their colleagues, workers, clients, and
consumers. They engage in economic activity for the sake
of the common good, and they experience this commitment as something transcending their self-interest, for the
benefit of present and future generations. Thus they work
not only for themselves, but also to ensure for others a
future and a dignified employment.

In the economic sector, states in particular need to
articulate policies of industrial and agricultural development concerned with social progress and the growth
everywhere of constitutional and democratic states. The
creation of ethical structures for currency, financial, and
commercial markets is also fundamental and indispensable;
these must be stabilized and better coordinated and con-
trolled so as not to prove harmful to the very poor. With
greater resolve than has hitherto been the case, the concern of peacemakers must also focus upon the food crisis,
which is graver than the financial crisis. The issue of food
security is once more central to the international political
agenda, as a result of interrelated crises, including sudden
shifts in the price of basic foodstuffs, irresponsible behavior

[5] Cf. ibid., 34 and 36: *AAS* 101 (2009), 668–70 and 671–72.

by some economic actors, and insufficient control on the part of governments and the international community. To face this crisis, peacemakers are called to work together in a spirit of solidarity, from the local to the international level, with the aim of enabling farmers, especially in small rural holdings, to carry out their activity in a dignified and sustainable way from the social, environmental, and economic points of view.

Education for a Culture of Peace: The Role of the Family and Institutions

6. I wish to reaffirm forcefully that the various peacemakers are called to cultivate a passion for the common good of the family and for social justice and a commitment to effective social education.

No one should ignore or underestimate the decisive role of the family, which is the basic cell of society from the demographic, ethical, pedagogical, economic, and political standpoints. The family has a natural vocation to promote life: it accompanies individuals as they mature, and it encourages mutual growth and enrichment through caring and sharing. The Christian family in particular serves as a seedbed for personal maturation according to the standards of divine love. The family is one of the indispensable social subjects for the achievement of a culture of peace. The rights of parents and their primary role in the education of their children in the area of morality and religion must be safeguarded. It is in the family that peacemakers, tomorrow's promoters of a culture of life and love, are born and nurtured.[6]

---

[6] Cf. John Paul II, *Message for the 1994 World Day of Peace* (December 8, 1993): *AAS* 86 (1994), 156–62.

Religious communities are involved in a special way in this immense task of education for peace. The Church believes that she shares in this great responsibility as part of the new evangelization, which is centered on conversion to the truth and love of Christ and, consequently, the spiritual and moral rebirth of individuals and societies. Encountering Jesus Christ shapes peacemakers, committing them to fellowship and to overcoming injustice.

Cultural institutions, schools, and universities have a special mission of peace. They are called to make a notable contribution not only to the formation of new generations of leaders, but also to the renewal of public institutions, both national and international. They can also contribute to a scientific reflection which will ground economic and financial activities on a solid anthropological and ethical basis. Today's world, especially the world of politics, needs to be sustained by fresh thinking and a new cultural synthesis so as to overcome purely technical approaches and to harmonize the various political currents with a view to the common good. The latter, seen as an ensemble of positive interpersonal and institutional relationships at the service of the integral growth of individuals and groups, is at the basis of all true education for peace.

A Pedagogy for Peacemakers

7. In the end, we see clearly the need to propose and promote a pedagogy of peace. This calls for a rich interior life, clear and valid moral points of reference, and appropriate attitudes and life-styles. Acts of peacemaking converge for the achievement of the common good; they create interest in peace and cultivate peace. Thoughts, words, and gestures of peace create a mentality and a culture of peace

and a respectful, honest, and cordial atmosphere. There is a need, then, to teach people to love one another, to cultivate peace, and to live with goodwill rather than mere tolerance. A fundamental encouragement to this is "to say no to revenge, to recognize injustices, to accept apologies without looking for them, and finally, to forgive",[7] in such a way that mistakes and offenses can be acknowledged in truth, so as to move forward together toward reconciliation. This requires the growth of a pedagogy of pardon. Evil is in fact overcome by good, and justice is to be sought in imitating God the Father who loves all his children (cf. Mt 5:21–48). This is a slow process, for it presupposes a spiritual evolution, an education in lofty values, a new vision of human history. There is a need to renounce that false peace promised by the idols of this world along with the dangers which accompany it, that false peace which dulls consciences, which leads to self-absorption, to a withered existence lived in indifference. The pedagogy of peace, on the other hand, implies activity, compassion, solidarity, courage, and perseverance.

Jesus embodied all these attitudes in his own life, even to the complete gift of himself, even to "losing his life" (cf. Mt 10:39; Lk 17:33; Jn 12:25). He promises his disciples that sooner or later they will make the extraordinary discovery to which I originally alluded, namely, that God is in the world, the God of Jesus, fully on the side of man. Here I would recall the prayer asking God to make us instruments of his peace, to be able to bring his love wherever there is hatred, his mercy wherever there is hurt, and true faith wherever there is doubt. For our part, let us join

---

[7] Benedict XVI, *Address at the Meeting with Members of the Government, Institutions of the Republic, the Diplomatic Corps, Religious Leaders and Representatives of the World of Culture*, Baabda-Lebanon (September 15, 2012): *L'Osservatore Romano*, September 16, 2012, p. 7.

Blessed John XXIII in asking God to enlighten all leaders so that, besides caring for the proper material welfare of their peoples, they may secure for them the precious gift of peace, break down the walls which divide them, strengthen the bonds of mutual love, grow in understanding, and pardon those who have done them wrong; in this way, by his power and inspiration, all the peoples of the earth will experience fraternity, and the peace for which they long will ever flourish and reign among them.[8]

With this prayer I express my hope that all will be true peacemakers, so that the city of man may grow in fraternal harmony, prosperity, and peace.

From the Vatican, December 8, 2012
BENEDICTUS PP XVI

---

[8] Cf. Encyclical Letter *Pacem in Terris* (April 11, 1963): *AAS* 55 (1963), 304.

X

Reason and Faith for a Common Ethics

A Dialogue with Jürgen Habermas
(January 19, 2004)

As the tempo of historical developments continues to accelerate around us, it seems to me that two factors are emerging as signs of a development that formerly proceeded only at a slow pace: on the one hand, the formation of a global society in which the individual political, economic, and cultural powers are increasingly interdependent and come into contact with one another in their different spheres of life and mutually interpenetrate. The other factor is the development of man's possibilities, of his power to make and to destroy, which raises the question of the legal and moral control of power in a way that goes far beyond anything customary until now. Thus it is a very urgent question, how cultures that encounter each other

From *Dialektik der Säkularisierung: Über Vernunft und Religion* (Freiburg im Breisgau: Herder, 2005). Previously published as "The Pre-political Moral Foundations of a Free State", trans. Michael J. Miller, in *Fundamental Speeches from Five Decades* (San Francisco: Ignatius Press, 2012), 201–15.

can find ethical foundations to guide their coexistence onto the right path and build a common, legally accountable structure that disciplines and orders power.

The fact that the "global ethic" project proposed by Hans Küng is in such demand shows in any case that the question has been framed. This is true even if one accepts the keen-sighted critique of this project that Robert Spaemann has offered.[1] For in addition to the two factors just mentioned, there is a third: as cultures encountered and interpenetrated each other, the ethical certainties that had previously upheld society were to a great extent shattered in the process. The basic question of what is actually good now, especially in the given context, and why one must do it, even to one's own detriment, remains largely unanswered.

Now it seems obvious to me that science as such cannot produce ethics and that therefore a renewed ethical awareness cannot come about as the product of scientific debates. On the other hand, it is also indisputable that the fundamental change in our view of the world and of man that has resulted from the growth in scientific knowledge plays an essential part in the shattering of old moral certainties. In this respect, science does have a responsibility for man as man, and philosophy in particular has a responsibility to accompany critically the development of the individual sciences, to shed a critical light on hasty conclusions and pseudo-certainties about what man is, where he comes from, and why he exists, or, to put it another way, to eliminate the nonscientific element from the scientific findings with which it is often mixed and, thus, to keep our perspective open to the totality, to the broader dimensions of the reality of human

[1] Robert Spaemann, "Weltethos als 'Projekt'", Merkur 570/571: 893–904.

existence, of which science can never manifest more than partial aspects.

1. POWER AND LAW

Specifically, it is the task of politics to put power under the moderating influence of the law and thus to order the sensible use of it. Not the law of the stronger, but the strength of the law must prevail. Power that is ordered by law and at its service is the antithesis of violence, by which we understand lawless and unlawful power. That is why it is important for every society to overcome suspicion of the law and of its ordinances, because only thereby can arbitrariness be banished and freedom be experienced as a commonly shared freedom. Lawless freedom is anarchy and, therefore, the destruction of freedom. Suspicion of the law, rebellion against the law, will always spring up when the law itself appears, no longer as the expression of a justice that is at the service of all, but, rather, as the result of arbitrariness and legislative arrogance on the part of those who have power. Hence the task of subjecting power to the criterion of law leads to the further question: How does law come into being, and how must law be constituted if it is to be a vehicle for justice and not the privilege of those who have the power to make the law? This poses, on the one hand, the question of the development of the law, but also, on the other hand, the question of its own intrinsic criteria. The law must not be an instrument of power wielded by a few but, rather, the expression of the common interest of all; this problem seems, initially at any rate, to be solved by the instruments of democratic consensus-building, because in them everyone collaborates in the development of the law, and, hence, it is everyone's law and can and must be respected as such. In fact, the guarantee of common collaboration in shaping the law and in the just administration of power is the essential argument in favor of democracy as the most suitable form of political order.

Despite this, it seems to me, another question remains. Since it is difficult to find unanimity among men, nothing is left for democratic consensus-building but the indispensable instruments of delegated authority, on the one hand, and majority rule, on the other hand, in which varying percentages can be required for a majority depending on the importance of the issue. But even majorities can be blind or unjust. History demonstrates this all too clearly. When a majority, however large, puts down a minority—a religious or racial minority, for instance—by oppressive laws, can one still speak about justice or about law at all? Thus the majority principle still leaves open the question of the ethical foundations of the law, the question of whether something exists that can never become law and, therefore, something that always remains wrong in itself or, conversely, something that by its nature is unalterably right, that is, prior to any majority vote, and must be respected by it.

The modern era has formulated a set of such normative elements in various declarations of human rights and put them beyond the reach of shifting majorities. Nowadays one may be content with the intrinsically self-evident character of these values, given the contemporary awareness of their importance. But even such a self-limitation of the inquiry has a philosophical character. There are, therefore, self-subsistent values that follow from the nature of being human and, hence, are inviolable for all who possess this nature. We will have to return again later to the operational range of this idea, especially since its self-evident character is by no means recognized in all cultures. Islam has defined its own catalogue of human rights, which differs from the Western list. Although China today is defined by a form of culture, Marxism, that originated in the West, some have informed me that it nevertheless raises the question of whether human rights are not a typically Western invention that must be scrutinized.

2. NEW FORMS OF POWER AND NEW QUESTIONS ABOUT MASTERING IT

In any discussion about the relation between power and law and about the sources of the law, a closer look must be taken at the phenomenon of power itself, also. Without trying to define the nature of power as such, I would like to sketch the challenges that result from the new forms of power that have developed in the last half century. The first phase of the period after World War II was dominated by alarm at the destructive power man had acquired with the invention of the atom bomb. Man suddenly saw himself in a position to destroy himself and the earth. This raised the question: What political mechanisms are necessary in order to ward off this destruction? How can such mechanisms be found and be made effective? How are we to mobilize the ethical forces that shape such political structures and make them work? Then, for a long period of time, it was de facto the competition between two opposing power blocs and the fear of bringing about one's own destruction with the destruction of the other that preserved us from the horrors of nuclear war. As it turned out, the reciprocal limitation of power and fear for one's own survival saved the day.

What makes us anxious these days is not so much fear of a large-scale war as fear of omnipresent terror that can strike and have its effect in any place. The human race, we see now, does not need a major war at all in order to make the world unlivable. The anonymous powers of terror, which can be present in all places, are strong enough to pursue everyone into the sphere of everyday life, whereby there is a lingering specter that criminal elements could gain access to weapons with great potential for destruction and thus deliver the world up to chaos apart from the political order. Thus the question about law and ethos has shifted: What are the sources on which terror feeds? How can this new sickness of mankind be eliminated successfully from within? The frightening thing about it is that terror, at least to some extent, claims moral legitimacy. Bin Laden's messages present terror as the response of the powerless, oppressed peoples to the haughtiness of the powerful, as the just punishment for their arrogance and for their blasphemous self-glorification and cruelty. For people in certain social and political situations, such motivations are evidently convincing. Sometimes terroristic behavior is depicted as the defense of religious tradition against the godlessness of Western society.

At this point a question arises, to which we must return later: If terrorism is fueled by religious fanaticism also—and it is—is religion then a healing, saving power, or is it not rather an archaic, dangerous power that sets up false, universalistic claims and thus leads astray to intolerance and terror? In that case, must not religion be placed under the guardianship of reason and be carefully restricted? Of course this also raises the question: Who can do that? How does one do that? But the general question remains: Should the gradual abolition of religion, the overcoming of religion, be regarded as necessary progress for mankind so that it can set out on the path of freedom and universal tolerance, or should it not?

Meanwhile, another form of power has come to the fore, which at first appears to be purely beneficent and thoroughly praiseworthy but in reality can lead to a new kind of threat to man. Man is now capable of making men, of growing them, so to speak, in a test tube. Man becomes a product, and with that the relation of man to himself is changed from top to bottom. He is no longer a gift of nature or of God the Creator; he is his own product. Man has descended into the springhouse of power, to the wellsprings of his own life. The temptation to construct man the right way at last, the temptation to experiment with men, the temptation to view men as garbage and to dispose of them, is not a mere figment of the imagination of some moralist opposed to progress.

Whereas earlier we considered the urgent question of whether religion really is a positive moral force, this now necessarily raises doubts about the reliability of reason. After all, the atom bomb, too, is ultimately a product of reason; ultimately the breeding and selection of men was devised by reason. Should not reason, therefore, in turn be placed under supervision now? But by whom or what? Or maybe religion and reason should limit each other reciprocally, each keeping the other within bounds and thus setting it on its positive path? At this juncture, the question again arises of how effective ethical clarity can be found in a global society with its mechanisms of power and with its unbridled forces as well as its different views of what constitutes law and morality: an ethics that has enough motivating force and persuasiveness to respond to the aforementioned challenges and to help deal with them.

3. PREREQUISITES FOR LAW: LAW—NATURE— REASON

First, this calls for a look at historical situations that are comparable to ours, to the extent that there is anything comparable. At any rate, it is worthwhile looking very briefly at the fact that ancient Greece had its own Enlightenment, that the divinely based law lost its self-evident character, and an inquiry into the deeper justifications of law became necessary. And so the idea occurred to someone: in contrast to positive law, which can be unjust, there must be a law that follows logically from the nature, the being of man himself. This law must be found, and then it will serve as a corrective to positive law.

A less remote example is the twofold break for the European consciousness that occurred at the beginning of the modern era and compelled it to seek new bases for reflection on the content and source of law. First, there was the emergence from the confines of the European, Christian world that was accomplished with the discovery of America. Europeans were now encountering peoples who did not belong to the Christian system of faith and law, which until then had been the source of law for everyone and had shaped it. There was no law in common with those peoples. But were they then lawless, as many maintained at that time (and to a great extent acted accordingly), or is there a law that goes beyond all legal systems and unites and guides men as men in their relations to each other? In this situation, Francisco de Vitoria developed the idea of the *ius gentium*, the "law of the nations", which was already current, whereby the connotation of "heathens", "non-Christians", is implied by the word *gentes*. This meant, therefore, the law that is prior to the Christian legal structure and is supposed to arrange a just coexistence of all peoples.

The second break in the Christian world took place within Christendom itself through schism, through which the community of Christians was compartmentalized into opposing and sometimes hostile communities. Again, a common law that was prior to dogma, at least the minimal legal requirement, had to be developed, the foundations of which now had to lie, not in faith, but rather in the nature of man, in human reason. Hugo Grotius, Samuel von Pufendorf, and others developed the idea of natural law as a rational law that transcends confessional boundaries and establishes reason as the instrument of the common legislative project.

Natural law—especially in the Catholic Church—has remained the argumentative approach with which Christianity appeals to common reason in dialogues with secular society and with other faith communities and seeks the foundations for an agreement about the ethical principles of law in a secular, pluralistic society. But this instrument, unfortunately, has become dull, and therefore I would rather not rely on it in this discussion. The idea of natural law presupposes a concept of nature in which nature and reason mesh and nature itself is rational. This view of nature has collapsed with the victory of evolutionary theory. Nature as such is not rational, even though there is rational behavior in it: that is the diagnosis we hear from that camp, and today it seems to a large extent incontrovertible.[2] Thus, of the various dimensions of the concept of nature underlying the natural law of former times, only one is left, which Ulpian (early third century A.D.)

---

[2] The philosophy of evolution, which is still dominant despite many corrections on individual points, is most impressively and consistently followed through in Jacques Monod, *Chance and Necessity: An Essay on the Natural Philosophy of Modern Biology* (New York, 1971). Helpful in distinguishing actual scientific findings from the accompanying philosophy is R. Junker and S. Scherer, eds., *Evolution: Ein kritisches Lehrbuch*, 4th ed. (Weyel, 1998). For references to the debate with the philosophy that accompanies the theory of evolution, see J. Ratzinger, *Truth and Tolerance: Christianity and World Religions*, trans. Henry Taylor (San Francisco: Ignatius Press, 2004), 162–83.

captured in the famous sentence: "Ius naturae est, quod natura omnia animalia docet" (The law of nature is what nature teaches all sentient beings).[3] But that very sentence is insufficient for our inquiries, which concern, not what is true of all *animalia*, but, rather, specifically human duties that man's reason has created and for which there could be no response without reason.

As the final element of the natural law, which at its deepest level intended to be a law of reason, in the modern era in any case, human rights have remained. They are not intelligible without the assumption that man as man, simply through his membership in the human species, is the subject of rights and that his very being bears within it values and norms that are to be discovered but not invented. Perhaps today the doctrine of human rights ought to be supplemented by a doctrine of human duties and human limits, and that could now help to revive the question of whether there might not be a reason of nature and thus a rational law for man and his standing in the world. Today such a discussion would have to be designed and carried out at an intercultural level. For Christians, it would have to do with creation and the Creator. In the Indian world, the corresponding concept would be that of "dharma",

[3] On the three dimensions of medieval natural law (dynamic of being in general, the directedness of the nature common to human beings and animals [Ulpian], the specific directedness of man's rational nature), cf. the references in the article by P. Delhaye, "Naturrecht", in *LThK*, 2nd ed., 8:821–25. The concept of natural law found at the beginning of the *Decretum Gratiani* is noteworthy: "Humanum genus duobus regitur, naturali videlicet jure, et moribus. Ius naturale est, quod in lege et Evangelio continetur, quo quisque iubetur alii facere quod sibi vult fieri et prohibetur alii inferre quod sibi nolit fieri" (The human race is governed by two things, namely, natural law and customs. The natural law is the one contained in the Law and the Gospel, whereby everybody is commanded to do unto others what he wishes to be done to himself and is forbidden to inflict on others what he does not wish to be done to himself).

the inner laws of being; and in the Chinese tradition, the idea of the ordinances of heaven.

4. INTERCULTURALITY AND ITS CONSEQUENCES

Before I try to draw conclusions, I would like to broaden a bit more the trail we have just blazed. Interculturality seems to me today to be an indispensable dimension for the discussion about the fundamental questions of human existence, which can be conducted neither as a merely intramural debate in Christianity nor merely within the Western rational tradition. In keeping with their self-understanding, both of these regard themselves as universal and may even be so de jure. De facto they must acknowledge that they are accepted only by parts of mankind and, furthermore, are comprehensible only in parts of mankind. The number of competing cultures is of course much smaller than it might seem at first glance.

The important thing, above all, is that there is no longer any uniformity within the cultural spheres; instead, all cultural spheres are characterized by far-reaching tensions within their own cultural tradition. In the West, this is quite obvious. Even though a strictly rational secular culture, of which Mr. Habermas gave us an impressive picture, is largely predominant and considers itself the element that binds people together, the Christian understanding of reality is now as ever an effective force. There are varying degrees of proximity or tension between the two poles; they may be willing to learn from each other or may have more or less decidedly rejected each other.

The Islamic cultural sphere, too, is characterized by similar tensions; there is a broad spectrum ranging from the fanatical absolutism of a Bin Laden to attitudes that are open to a tolerant rationality. The third great cultural sphere, Indian culture, or, more precisely, the cultural spheres of

Hinduism and Buddhism, are again marked by similar tensions, even though they appear less dramatic, at least to our eyes. These cultures, too, find that they are exposed to the claim of Western rationality and also to the inquiries of the Christian faith, which are both present within them; they assimilate the one and the other in different ways while seeking to maintain their own identity. The tribal cultures of Africa and the tribal cultures of Latin America that have been reawakened by certain Christian theologies complete the picture. They appear to a great extent to call Western rationality into question but also to question the universal claim of Christian revelation.

What can we conclude from all this? First, it seems to me, the two great cultures of the West, the culture of Christian faith and that of secular rationality, are in fact not universal, however influential they both may be, each in its own way, throughout the world and in all cultures. In this respect, the question of the colleague from Teheran mentioned by Mr. Habermas seems to me to be of some importance, after all: namely, the question of whether the sociology of religion and a comparative study of cultures might not suggest that European secularization is an exceptional path in need of correction. I would not unconditionally, at least not necessarily, reduce this question to the state of mind of Carl Schmitt, Martin Heidegger, and Lévi-Strauss—that of a European situation weary of rationality, so to speak. The fact is, in any case, that our secular rationality, however obvious it is to our Western-trained reason, does not make sense to every *ratio* and that in its attempt to make itself evident, as rationality, it runs into its limitations. Its self-evidence is in fact bound up with definite cultural contexts, and, that being the case, it must acknowledge that it cannot be reproduced in mankind as a whole and, hence, cannot be wholly operative in it, either. In other words, the rational or the ethical or the religious formula of the world on which everyone agreed and which then could support the whole does not exist. In any case, it is presently unattainable. That is why even the so-called world ethic remains an abstraction.

5. CONCLUSIONS

What is to be done, then? With regard to the practical consequences, I find myself largely in agreement with the remarks of Mr. Habermas about a post-secular society and about a willingness to learn and self-limitation on both sides. To conclude this lecture, I would like to summarize my own view in two theses.

1. We have seen that there are pathologies in religion that are extremely dangerous and that make it necessary to regard the divine light of reason, so to speak, as a regulatory body; religion must again and again be purified and ordered anew in terms of reason—which, incidentally, was also the idea of the Church Fathers.[4] But our reflections also showed that, although mankind in general is not as aware of it, there are also pathologies of reason, a *hubris* of reason that is no less dangerous but even more menacing in terms of its potential efficiency: atom bomb, man as product. That is why, conversely, reason, too, must be reminded about its limits and must learn to be willing to listen to the great religious traditions of mankind. If it completely emancipates itself and rejects this willingness to learn and this correlative status, it becomes destructive.

Kurt Hübner recently formulated a similar demand and said that such a thesis does not directly involve a "return to faith" but, rather, is a matter of "being liberated from

---

[4] I tried to describe this in more detail in my book *Truth and Tolerance*, which was mentioned in n. 2; cf. also M. Fiedrowicz, *Apologie im frühen Christentum*, 2nd ed. (Schöningh, 2001).

the momentous delusion that it (that is, faith) has nothing more to say to contemporary man because it contradicts one's humanistic idea of reason, enlightenment, and
freedom."[5] Accordingly, I would speak about a necessary
relatedness between reason and faith, reason and religion,
which are called to purify and heal each other; they need
each other and must recognize each other.

2. This basic rule must then find concrete expression in
practice, in the intercultural context of the present day.
No doubt the two main partners in this mutual relatedness
are Christian faith and Western secular rationality. This can
and must be said without any false Euro-centrism. The two
determine the world situation to an extent unequalled by
any other cultural force. But that does not mean that one
could set the other cultures aside as a sort of "negligi-
ble quantity". That would indeed be a sort of Western
hubris, and we would pay dearly for it—to some extent
we are already paying the price. It is important for these
two major components of Western culture to assume an
attitude of listening and to enter into a true relatedness
with these cultures as well. It is important to include them
in the attempt at a polyphonic relatedness, in which they
open themselves to the essential complementariness of reason and faith, so that a universal process of purifications
can develop, in which the essential values and norms that
are somehow known or sensed by all men can finally gain
new illuminating power, so that what holds the world
together can again become an effective force in mankind.

[5] K. Hübner, *Das Christentum im Wettstreit der Religionen* (Mohr Siebeck,
2003), 148.

XI

Does God Exist?

A Debate of Joseph Ratzinger with Paolo Flores d'Arcais (September 21, 2000)

Gad Lerner: Good evening, everybody. Thank you for coming. The first thing I must ask, in the name of the title of this debate, is to turn off your cell phones, please. The ring tones would clash somewhat with this question, with this rather unseemly title that we are addressing this evening: *Does God exist?* An unseemly title for a debate organized by a Christian and by an atheist, which, due to a perhaps not entirely random coincidence, is being moderated by a Jew and, in the brutality of the question that is posed, may resemble some medieval disputations rather than our more or less superficial televised conversations.

Naturally this is a question that causes our veins to throb when it is posed in public and so directly. But our starting point—which I summarized brutally in the introduction of our speakers by referring to them as the Christian and

This text is the transcript of the video-recorded dialogue between Joseph Ratzinger and Paolo Flores d'Arcais in a debate entitled *Dio esiste?*, moderated by Gad Lerner, which was held in the Teatro Quirino in Rome on September 21, 2000. English translation of the Italian transcript by Michael J. Miller.

the atheist, otherwise known as His Eminence Joseph Cardinal Ratzinger, prefect of the Congregation for the Doctrine of the Faith, and Paolo Flores d'Arcais, philosopher and editor of [the bi-monthly Roman news magazine] *MicroMega*—could also be formulated with the descriptions "believer" and "nonbeliever", which I believe are accepted no doubt by both. Are the boundaries between someone who believes and someone who does not believe really so neat and clear within you—I mean, besides in our society today? I do not find them clear at all. Are we quite sure that between these two interlocutors there are not instead some significant traits in common, too? We will listen to them presently.

My only remaining task is to remind you that this debate took its cue from issue number 2 of *MicroMega* in the year 2000, which had—and this cannot be by chance—a truly extraordinary success, not only in the interest that it has attracted but also, as you know, in sales, if it is true that with the latest reprinted edition it has actually managed to reach one hundred thousand copies sold. It will really mean something also in terms of the need for discussion experienced by believers and nonbelievers, by Christians and atheists. And so, between our two speakers, to whom I will immediately give the floor, perhaps we can quickly identify a common trait, which in some way makes their mutual intransigence symmetrical if not exactly common. And this is, on both sides, the rejection of a religiosity of convenience, the rejection of a God made to measure, tailor-made by each person for himself, through care for his own body and his own soul, without thinking much of others or of what is transcendent, that is, without fully coming to terms with the problem of truth.

This kind of convenient religiosity is very widespread, as you know. The label that it takes in our opulent societies, most of the time, is "New Age" or else a certain idea of Buddhism. The relativism that inspires it is vehemently criticized by both my interlocutors in the texts they published in *MicroMega*, and above all, therefore, there is in them this need to come to terms with the absolute of truth. But in giving the floor to this debate, I would like to ask them also: starting as they do from such distant points of view, what then gives rise to the reciprocal need to speak to each other: From what does it spring? I ask first of all His Eminence Cardinal Ratzinger.

Joseph Ratzinger: It springs from the fact that we believers think we have something to say to the world, to others, that the question of God is not just a private question of our little club that has its interest, plays its game, does its thing, but, rather, we are convinced that man needs to know God; we are convinced that in Jesus the truth appeared, and the truth is a thing that is not each person's private property but must be shared, must be known. And therefore we are convinced that precisely at this moment of history, of the religious crisis and also of the crisis of the major cultures in their encounter [with one another], it is important that we not live only inside the little world of our purchases and personal living arrangements but really be exposed to the questions of others, and that, by this availability and this frankness, we make others understand what seems to us to be reasonable or, indeed, necessary for man. *we all need to know God = truth appears*

Lerner: Paolo Flores d'Arcais: "reasonable and necessary". God is, the faith is reasonable and necessary for man, says Cardinal Ratzinger, who in his essay, too, which was published in *MicroMega*, insists on the rationality, if I can put it that way, of Christianity.

Paolo Flores d'Arcais: In a debate of this kind there is a major asymmetry, because the believer is interested in converting the nonbeliever (he is "interested" in the highest sense of the term, obviously). The atheist is definitely not interested in convincing the believer about the nonexistence of God; he has no interest in making anyone lose his faith. Well, then, why is an atheist, too, profoundly interested in faith and in the type of faith, especially of those who practice it? Because to be an atheist (a word that some consider to be in bad taste—but why should we not state the fact soberly?) simply means to maintain that everything plays out here, in our finite, uncertain existence. And therefore that what counts are the values that are chosen in this life, the consistency between the values that are chosen and one's own conduct, and, on the basis of this—precisely because everything plays out here, within the horizon of this life—the alliances and forms of solidarity that are established, the conflicts and encounters that occur.

And then, precisely from the perspective of the values that are chosen, and especially of the possibility of a kind of coexistence based on tolerance, that is, on mutual respect, the type of faith is not an indifferent matter. If the faith of a Christian is that of the first generations of Christians, it is summed up in a phrase—we do not know who actually pronounced it (even though it is attributed to Tertullian, it is not found in the writings of any author), but the concept is quite clear in Saint Paul also: "Credo quia absurdum" (I believe because it is absurd), that is, the faith is a scandal for reason.

If faith is this, then no conflict arises with the nonbeliever, because a faith of this kind will not claim to impose itself; it will ask only to be respected.

But if the Catholic faith claims to be the summary and the fulfillment of reason, that is, claims to be the summary

and the fulfillment of what is most characteristic of man
and, therefore, to be truly the *summa* of reason and
humanity, then you know that if faith claims to be that,
the risk that it might then be tempted to impose itself—
even through the secular arm of the state—is inevitable,
because anyone who was in conflict with the dictates of
the faith and above all with its moral consequences would
also be "anti-reason" and "anti-humanity".

Lerner: Excuse me, Flores, we may be getting ahead of ourselves if we start talking about the secular arm of the state.
You asked what I think is a decisive question, which moreover was presented also in your essay, namely: But why
do you believers, you Christians, you men of faith, not
give up the worldly demonstration of the truth, because
you claim to give rational garb also to something that is
plainly absurd? If you were to accept, Flores says (attributing it also to early Christianity, although I do not know
if you [*turning to Ratzinger*] will agree—you [*turning again
to Ratzinger*] will probably dispute this thesis of his), if
you were to accept the idea of the absurdity of the faith,
well, we would be satisfied, we would let you believe, we
would let you believe because you are free to do so, but
on the whole we would be content with the fact that the
absurdity of this faith was known and verified.

Ratzinger: In reality, I am convinced that the first generations of Christianity did not think of the absurdity of the
faith. It is true, Paul speaks about the "scandal", and we see
that this scandal exists in all generations, even today, but
at the same time he preaches in the Areopagus, the center
of ancient culture and ancient philosophy, in a discussion
with the philosophers, and he even cites the philosophers. And generally the beginning of Christian preaching

addressed the so-called *phoboumenoi theon* [Greek: "the God-fearing"], that is, the groups of persons who had formed around the synagogue. Judaism had a very important function and position in the ancient world, inasmuch as this faith in one God the Creator appeared precisely as the rational religion that was being sought at the time of the crisis of the gods. And therefore this religion was offered as a true, authentic religion, not invented by the philosophers, but really born in the heart of man and from the light of God, and, on the other hand, corresponding deeply to the rational convictions of that period and therefore of persons of that period who were—let us say—enlightened, in search of God and no longer content with the state religions, persons who were seeking a religion that is authentically religion, not only a philosophical construction, but also in keeping with reason.

These persons had created a circle around the synagogue, and that was the world where Paul could preach. And his intention and his conviction was really this one God who spoke with Abraham, who spoke in the Old Testament and who now makes himself seen and accessible through Jesus to the peoples of the world, and therefore, realizing that, on the one hand, he was giving scandal in the Areopagus, we see the proclamation of the Resurrection that creates a scandal. He was also convinced that he was not proclaiming something absurd that pleases some but was bringing with him a message that could appeal to human reason and tell people: we are all seeking God in this moment of crisis, we are seeking a religion that is not invented but authentic and, on the other hand, is consonant with our reason. And Saint Peter, in his First Letter, says explicitly that you must always be prepared to give a reason for your hope. You must always *apologein*, give an account of the *logos*. In other words, they must be ready to demonstrate the *logos*, the profoundly rational sense of their convictions.

Therefore, it is true—on this point I am naturally in agreement with Professor Flores d'Arcais—that this must not be imposed. An appeal is made to conscience and to reason: this is the only authority that can decide. It really is a sin to think: then if reason is not ready, we must "help" it, in quotation marks, with the power of the state. This is a major error. But therefore [faith must] not assert itself with power—that is a great sin and error—but, rather, present itself to the clarity of reason and of the heart.

Flores d'Arcais: But of course Christianity succeeds in asserting itself in a context of the crisis of the traditional religions, and in a preparation—by many philosophical schools, too—for a religion of a different type, based on one God. And nevertheless it seems clear to me, reading the texts, that for the first generations of Christians, reason was not what led them to believe, but faith: indeed, *essentially* in contrast with what seemed to the people of that time to be reason.

Paul uses an expression that I think must be taken literally: the "folly of the cross". This is what differentiates Christianity from Plato or from many other philosophical schools, including Epicurus—even Epicurus believed in God, in a God, however, who was totally indifferent to the destiny of mankind. What characterizes Christianity and what Paul repeats constantly is not simply faith in one God, it is faith in Jesus Christ who died and rose again.

The Resurrection is the essential key, the specific difference of the Christian religion. And in his famous debate with the philosophers in the Areopagus, it is no accident that—as the Acts of the Apostles relate—as long as they discussed God, a God who was one, the discussion went on. As soon as there was talk about the resurrection of the dead, everyone went away, not even scandalized or incredulous, but simply bored. Because that truly seemed to be folly for reason.

So the essential element, if we do not want to reduce Christianity to one of the many philosophy-religions of that era, is precisely this folly for reason, the folly of the Cross, of the Resurrection, the insistence on the theme of the resurrection of the dead, of bodily resurrection. All this, in my view, shows that it is necessary to affirm faith as a right that, however, is in contrast with reason, and there is no ...

Lerner: Excuse me, Professor, I have a specific question to ask you about faith, but perhaps Cardinal Ratzinger wishes to respond to you about this observation ...

Ratzinger: Yes ...

Lerner: The Resurrection, the folly of the Resurrection as the central element of the Christian faith.

Ratzinger: Yes. So, the first point is that Saint Paul is convinced that it is something that appeals to reason, but he is also convinced that it goes beyond the things evident to reason because, as I understand Saint Paul, love is involved, love that is not anti-rational but far exceeds reason.

And this God who is *logos* (as Saint John then says), who is creative reason, who is Word—because *logos* is not simply reason but is already a reason that speaks, that is, one that relates and draws near; thus we have already a renewal of the concept of reason that goes beyond the pure mathematics, the pure geometry of being—nevertheless it is *logos*, and even when speaking and even when going beyond this pure mathematics, it nevertheless remains *logos*, that is, reasonable. It is—and here the fact that it is love is already proclaimed—someone who draws near, and really this love does some foolish things: for a God it appears absurd if from his eternal happiness he draws near to this tiny creature that is man and comes into play in this world even to death.

This contrasts radically with the purely philosophical concept of God, and Paul is well aware of this contrast, but nevertheless he makes us understand that it is ultimately the freedom, the greatness of the highest reason to be love, too, and then therefore to exceed the limits that our philosophical speculation might set on this divinity.

And another note: to me it seems very significant that the first two, three, or four centuries of Christianity, when seeking a connection with the surrounding culture, never connected with the religions, they were not seen on the track of the religions but said: our religion is a continuation and fulfillment of the philosophies and even goes beyond them, but it sees in philosophy the pre-presence of Christ, of the *Logos* in the world.

And thus the self-definition of these first generations was precisely this: we are not one religion like many others, we have the same rights as the other religions, but we are the continuation of the human thought that criticized the religions, that found a trail of God, but naturally could not really identify him by its own power. And the novelty of Christianity according to these Fathers is that that same hidden, conjectured God manifests himself and naturally then radically exceeds what could be seen and, nevertheless, proves to be in unity with this human search.

Lerner: There you have it. At this point, naturally, the temptation would be to pursue the question that, however,

Cardinal Ratzinger answers in his text, about how and why Christianity became a world religion. It is not the only one, as you know: there is also Islam from this perspective, in a later phase. But there can be interpretations of a historical character and of a character that is instead providential, or both intertwined. But let's get to that later, because first I feel obliged to make an attempt to "draw out" Flores.

Flores d'Arcais: But I have a response ...

Lerner: But you have a question even before a response, because there is a question precisely because of the crucial character of the topic that we have selected, which is the topic of the faith from which the atheist, Paolo Flores d'Arcais, cannot flee, and that is: Can one live without faith? More precisely, I would like here to use the arguments of my theologian friend Enzo Bianchi, published in the same issue of *MicroMega*, which I share entirely, in which he speaks about faith as an anthropological datum, as an existential datum of the human being. One can certainly live without a religious faith, but not without some form of reliance on faith. Having known Paolo Flores d'Arcais for many years, I am convinced that in his own way he is a man of faith. Do we want to deal with this reality?

Flores d'Arcais: Certainly. First two words in response to the most recent remarks by Cardinal Ratzinger.

In Saint Paul's writings, we find many times the claim that reason can arrive at God—and certainly this was his debate with the philosophers, too—but never that what is distinctive about Christianity, namely, faith in the risen Christ, can be proved by reason. On the other hand, if it were not so, faith would not be a gift, faith would be something within the reach of everyone's reason.

The claim that Christianity is the fulfillment and not the antithesis of the great philosophies of the early centuries—of those that we now call the first centuries of the Christian era—is affirmed completely when we come to Saint Augustine. And Saint Augustine would be the fundamental element of the Christian tradition that followed. But with Saint Augustine, we are a few generations after the first generations, and, not by chance—alas and tragically—Saint Augustine is also the first great figure of Christianity who, breaking with a tradition that seemed to be consolidated, considers it necessary and desirable, in the latter part of his life—contradicting also the first part of it—for convictions and conversions to be assisted by the severity, as he says, of the intervention of the secular arm, opening a tragic chapter in the history of humanity.

As for Gad Lerner's question: Can one live without faith? It is enough to agree about the word "faith". If by faith you mean any deep, existential passion for some values, precisely the things that make one's own existence and one's own relation with others something meaningful, then no. But that would indeed be an incredibly generic definition of faith.

If by faith you mean instead a religious belief, I calmly answer yes: one can live without faith. Faith is quite unnecessary to give meaning to one's own existence; one can give meaning to one's own existence in many ways.

Pascal, the greatest Christian thinker of the modern era, used this argument to state his idea of the wager: God, the existence of the soul, and so on, cannot be proved in exclusively human terms (in his writings, too, there is this element of something in faith that is irreducible to reason and that can even be in conflict with it). And therefore to his skeptical friends of that era, he spoke about a rich world that was accustomed to playing games of chance. Try to wager: What is worth betting on, your immortality and the truth of the Catholic religion, or the fact that there is nothing more after this life? His reasoning, as you know, was: Basically, if there is nothing after this life, what have you lost by betting on immortality? Nothing. But if there is something after this life, then by betting on mortality you have lost everything. Look, in this reasoning there is an element that does not work: it is not true that by having faith one has only something more and loses nothing; I think that faith is certainly something more in terms of hope or illusion ...

Lerner: "One more step", our current president of the [Italian] Council [of Ministers, Giuliano Amato,] said.

Flores d'Arcais: Yes, but it also brings something less, because I believe that lucidity and the awareness of finiteness and of disenchantment allow us to live passionately and more responsibly the everyday events of our one little life.

Lerner: Your Eminence, in your view can there be any common feature between faith understood as civil commitment, militant passion, acting according to one's own ideals (as the atheist Flores d'Arcais has pointed out), and faith in God?

Ratzinger: No doubt I see common ground. Naturally, I would say that mere formal militancy without contents, by itself, is not a good thing. This is about some contents, is it not? One can be very fervently militant for a very bad cause, and that alone does not make it good. But I would say that there can be fundamental convictions about values that support life and also dignified coexistence in this world, and here, to quote his words, we can be militant together. I would say: to fight intolerance, the types of fanaticism that always recur. And then commitment to human dignity, to freedom, to generosity toward the poor and the needy.

It seems to me that, in this world of ours, there are values that we share: they—the atheists—and we believers. And it seems to be of the utmost importance that, notwithstanding this deep division that exists between faith, in the sense of Christian faith, and atheism, that we are on terrain on which we have a common responsibility.

Perhaps the atheist is offended that we think that these values ultimately come from the conviction that being itself carries within it a moral message, which in itself is not neutral but shows us a direction toward love and against hatred, toward truth and against falsehood. That this direction, already inherent in being, results from the origin of being, from God, and therefore we think that ultimately this conviction and also the commitment to the values of humanity and of human dignity result from a hidden presence of that which we cannot manipulate. And in this sense also, it would be an expression of a deeper faith, even if not defined in theological terms.

It seems to me quite logical that we can think this, while still respecting the fact that the atheist does not see this and maybe also disputes this common root that nourishes commitments to the good and against evil.

Lerner: But Your Eminence, how much you have allowed yourselves, as a Church, to be contaminated by laicist, Enlightenment thinking! You used here, a few moments ago, the word "intolerance", and this seemed normal to us. Less normal perhaps is the fact that this very word "intolerance" appeared on March 12 of this year in the Lenten liturgy, in the prayer of the pope in Saint Peter's, as part of that liturgy of purification of memory for the sins committed by the sons of the Church in her name. But this word and this concept, "tolerance", like "intolerance", which originated in the Enlightenment era and belong intensely to laicist and Enlightenment thought, have entered, of all things, into the discourse of the prefect of the Congregation for the Doctrine of the Faith, and even more, I might say, into the prayers of the pope in Saint Peter's.

This contamination exists, therefore; is it fortunate, is it positive, do you accept it, or does it worry you a bit? You are considered a very severe man.

Ratzinger: Well, I would say two things. Laicist thought, Enlightenment thought: these are concepts that need to be defined. In Italy the adjective *laico* (lay) is understood in contrast to the adjective *credente* (believing), which is not the case in other languages. Therefore, this concept of laicism for me is not as transparent as it may appear to be here. The *illuminista* (Enlightenment) opinion, too: in a conference given at the Sorbonne, I sought to show that Christianity intended to be a kind of enlightenment along the lines of Socrates, too, and especially of the Old Testament prophets, who were true *illuministi* (promoters of enlightenment) with regard to the worship of idols: and therefore Christianity intended to be in a certain sense a kind of enlightenment, too ...

Lerner: But allow me to say: although Christianity and the Enlightenment sounded to you like sacred reason, they have had a rather bloody clash.

Ratzinger: Yes, because twins can also clash with each other. At a certain time in history, two very different modes developed: a Christianity that was rather self-enclosed, forgetting somewhat its "enlightenment" heritage—so to speak, in a broader sense than that of the period about which you are talking—and another mode that consequently is opposed to Christianity and considers it obscurantism.

I think that the time has come to transcend these oppositions. The Enlightenment that arose in certain circumstances, in the 1700 and 1800s, was an enlightenment opposed to Christianity, although not in every respect. There were also—I could also give names—currents of Christian Enlightenment in that era. Unfortunately, these conciliatory tendencies seeking a common path did not prevail, but they existed just the same, and, on the other hand, Christianity ought to think again about these roots that it has. So I do not see an absolute opposition, even though I see an opposition between certain features of the modern Enlightenment and the Christian faith.

Therefore, I would not speak here about contamination, because it is understood that "contamination" implies something dirty, and we certainly do not mean that. On the contrary, I say: it seems to me to be a very positive thing that these two currents that had separated, and to a certain extent will probably be separate in the future, also, nevertheless meet and fructify each other, and one begins to learn from the other.

Lerner: I have to clarify that the word "contamination" can be used also in a positive way. It was not my intention to use it in the negative sense. This is very interesting, Flores: Maybe we are scarcely acquainted with a Cardinal Ratzinger who is much less rigid than the one we imagined, or am I wrong?

Flores d'Arcais: Here there are two topics or questions; I will reply starting with the latter, and then we can turn to the first one (the common ground). I am sorry that I do not have here the volume with all the encyclicals of Karol Wojtyła, which is one of my favorite things to read, because on almost every page I can find and read quotations explicitly and virulently criticizing Enlightenment thought. Moreover, the thought of Karol Wojtyła that we are considering ...

Lerner: Why do you call him that?

Flores d'Arcais: Karol Wojtyła?

Lerner: May I ask you why? You do not use his title as pope, John Paul II.

Flores d'Arcais: I use indiscriminately either Karol Wojtyła or Pope Wojtyła, or John Paul II or "the current pontiff". When I write, I use these expressions indiscriminately because, as everyone knows, in a good Italian style you need to avoid repetitions. And in speaking, because it happens.

Well, then, in the thought of John Paul II, we are accustomed to underline throughout one period the critique of Communism above all and, in a second period, after the fall of the [Berlin] Wall, the critique of unbridled liberalism and hedonistic consumerism (hence of the bourgeois world under this aspect). In reality, if we indeed read the pope's encyclicals attentively, we will find practically—from his first encyclical on—that Karol Wojtyła had already identified these two elements as his critical objectives, because—and we read this in all his encyclicals, I would say that it is the constant of his philosophy—he saw in Communism and in hedonism and bourgeois consumerist individualism two facets of the same reality, two different sons of the modern Enlightenment. This is the fundamental element. For this reason, let us say that the essential element of this pope, in terms of his philosophical ideas, is exactly that the individualism that arises with the Enlightenment initiates this loss of the idea of Truth with a capital T, which he considers the root of all the disasters of the following centuries. Indeed, in more than one passage, this pontiff maintains—though he is neither the first nor the only one—that the major tragedies of this century, namely, the Nazi concentration camps and the repressions of the Soviet gulag, and therefore the great mass exterminations in the name of both ideologies, have their roots precisely in the Enlightenment with its invention of the primacy of the individual. This is so true that I have had occasion to write that Wojtyła in particular ends up seeing Voltaire as the root of all the evils of the modern era.

These things can actually be found in print, and for this reason it is a great pleasure for me to hear Cardinal Ratzinger pronounce the words that he pronounced today. But since I take no pleasure in the game that many play, of thinking that the prefect of the Congregation for the Doctrine of the Faith is then in disagreement with the pope—these are little games that should be left to others— I am convinced that in reality, when he says: there is a good enlightenment and a bad enlightenment, he then ends up saying that the bad enlightenment is the one that we know as the Enlightenment, that is, the Voltairian and post-Voltairian tradition, and by good enlightenment he means something that is almost undetectable historically or in a very small minority and that the question is the individual. But since the first question was about common ground, I only mention it, because we will discuss it.

Lerner: Don't you want to hear first the response to this?

Flores d'Arcais: No, I would like first to put ... Seeing that there has been talk about this, too ...

I think that there is a common ground. The common ground can be something that for Catholics should be the ABC's (and therefore the common ground ought to be very easy). I think that the common ground could consist of the Gospel and the values of the Gospel, especially two values that I consider truly fundamental, namely: "Let your yes be yes, and your no, no, because anything more comes from the evil one", which, as you know, is not only a terrible indictment of hypocrisy but something infinitely more than that. It is the idea that all diplomacy, that every additional word with respect to a radical *aut* [Latin: either/or] is the work of the devil.

I would be extremely pleased if not only all laicists and the atheists but all Christians reasoned in these terms. And then there are countless passages of the Gospel that in practice consider the sin of all sins to be privilege and inequality of wealth.

Look, I think that starting from these two values it could be very easy to reach an understanding. I have the impression that these two values, often, are perceived much more by many who are not believers than by the majority of believers. [*Loud applause.*]

Lerner: As I feared, despite the great success of this speech of yours, it would have been better if you had been interrupted earlier, because this way we are mixing two levels of discussion that were more useful ...

Flores d'Arcais: But in his speech, the cardinal ...

Lerner: Of course, you are free. But I, if you agree, would keep them separate. I think that it would be very interesting for Cardinal Ratzinger to respond to the question about the interpretations of enlightenment, because this is a decisive point. And then, in a second step, we could get to the arguments about possible meeting grounds. Please.

Ratzinger: Yes. I am not prepared now to interpret in depth the pope's encyclicals (*smiles*), because it is a large body of writing that must be studied carefully. It is true that the Holy Father has criticized, and does criticize equally, on the one hand, Communism, as a form of totalitarianism that destroyed not only the ecology, the earth, but also souls, and, on the other hand, also the dangers of liberal civilization.

It seems to me that it should not be so difficult to share the substance of these criticisms. The Holy Father had experienced that regime and, above all, the falsehood that was the true characteristic of that regime. Many bishops, priests, and simple lay people tell me, above all and even from former-Communist Germany: "Our real problem was the falsehood. No one trusted the other person anymore, no one dared to speak the truth. We all lived under that pressure, in a dictatorship of falsehood and of mutual hypocrisy. And so we were ruined, not just physically, but in our souls." And true liberation ought to be precisely liberation from this dictatorship of hypocrisy and falsehood.

On the other hand, the pope also criticizes our Western civilization, and some say that he is now the last apologist for ideal socialism, which defends the ideals of socialism against an exaggerated individualism and against all the evils that result from it. And, it seems to me, the criticism of our present civilization, in which we are all grateful for our freedom, grateful also for our well-being, is nevertheless a necessary thing, and we see in liberalism the real growth of a lack of sensitivity to the other, a centrality of the ego, a centrality of material and superficial things that, likewise, become a deterioration and an impoverishment of our souls.

And therefore critiquing this civilization of ours—which has its valuable points, which we know well—no one wants this to happen now, through some speech or another. Nevertheless, it is a need shared by many minds that are, I would say, enlightened.

Now Professor Flores d'Arcais tells me that these two criticisms, which are, let us say, somewhat contrasting but complementary, are, according to the pope, merely variations on the criticism of the Enlightenment as such, which is supposedly considered to be individualism and the root of all the evils of our time. I said that now I do not dare to discuss the authenticity of his interpretation of the pope, but I am convinced that, in the pope's view, Communism does not have the same root and is not likewise rooted in the nineteenth-century Enlightenment, like liberal culture, which nevertheless also does not grow automatically into its present pernicious forms from that root but develops with a new automatism, due to totally new factors.

It is not true that nothing new arises in history. In our century, and in the past century, totally new factors entered the picture that cannot simply be reduced to Voltaire's thought. From these intellectual currents come negative elements that caused humanity to begin to lose respect for man; it seems to me that the history of our century proves it already in the cruelty of World War I. And therefore, self-criticism on the part of the Enlightenment, about itself, about the problems created by the loss of values that appeared to be—let us say—threats to freedom ... such self-criticism, such an examination of the Enlightenment conscience would not seem useless to me.

I am glad to see and hear the applause confirming the superiority of nonbelievers over believers in regard to their fidelity to the Gospel. Nevertheless—it seems to me—it is always good for us believers, and also for nonbelievers, to be self-critical, to reflect on the dangers of our own position; and therefore, without attributing the evils of our century—which do not grow automatically from the nineteenth century—to this Enlightenment, to be, let us say ... thoughtful also about this heritage and to have the courage to question ourselves, to reflect once again in depth—this, it seems to me, would be a very important thing and also something that could be an element in common between the two parties.

Lerner: Here, I lose my balance [that is, momentarily forsake the neutrality of a moderator], and I applaud, too, because I am convinced that it is a sign of great wisdom for everyone to applaud especially something that startles us, makes us reflect, raises doubts in us rather than whatever simply reassures us. This seems to me a good point of common life to keep.

But I would take advantage, Your Eminence, of the fact that you made these references also to self-criticism in order to pose to you a question that for me is crucial, especially in the course of this Jubilee Year, the Christian Bimillennium, during which there is no doubt that the moment of purification of memory, the so-called *mea culpa*, was very important compared with the jubilees of the past.

Look, for us who are not Christians, it is rather simple to historicize, to relativize forms of conduct, to explain the Crusades, the Inquisition, the imposition of forced conversion on populations, by pointing to the mentality of the era, the conflicts, the pressures, the tensions, the cultures of the era. We are prone to historicize and relativize, but the Church—the Church that thinks of herself as a supra-temporal entity that goes through history but is somehow immanent to it—how can she explain to herself these sins, these faults of the past? Is it not a philosophical simplification, I would say, to attribute them simply to men who committed them in her name, while remaining the infallible, pure Church?

Flores d'Arcais: Would it not be better for me to respond first to the first question? Otherwise, it is my turn, then, to answer two questions and to be long-winded and boring.

Well, then. Certainly this pope will go down in history. Besides the fact that, for many other reasons he will go down in Church history, or simply in history, because of the fundamental role that he played against Communist totalitarianism. This remains a fact and, indeed, the anti-totalitarian commitment of this pope was the commitment of a solid part of the Polish Church before Karol Wojtyła, archbishop of Krakow, became pope.

I recall that a very dear Polish friend of mine, Adam Michnik, who was one of the leaders of the dissent in Poland and for this reason spent his youth in and out of jail, although he was a nonbeliever, coming from the heretical Communist dissenters, for a long time found hospitality for his writing, obviously with a pseudonym, only in a Catholic weekly, *Tygodnik Powszechny*, which was sponsored by Karol Wojtyła and edited by a theologian who was among his dearest friends. Therefore, the anti-totalitarian commitment of this pope is part of his whole life, not only of his papacy.

Nevertheless, these criticisms of totalitarianism and then of unbridled consumerist hedonism, which of course are quite fine with me—I think that there should be some consistency to them. If anything, the criticism that I hear myself making of this pope is that then he does not remain consistent in this criticism and, I don't think it is by chance, for reasons precisely of his anti-Enlightenment position. Why?

After the defeat of Communism in Poland, and therefore of the totalitarianism that claimed to impose by law on consciences something that did not sit well with some consciences—it really is of no importance whether they were in the majority or in the minority—once democracy was reestablished in Poland, the pope sought to impose, by law, a series of Christian values that another part of the citizenship did not share.

In this very same volume of *MicroMega*, there is an essay by a philosopher who has very close ties to the pope, his personal friend Leszek Kołakowski—Cardinal Ratzinger surely knows him—who is systematically invited every two years to the reserved meetings that the pope has with a group of scientists and philosophers to discuss major questions in private and who is therefore considered by the Christian world and by the Church to be a reference point. And yet this thinker, Leszek Kołakowski, writes an article—each one of you can read it, and so you will see that it is not just an interpretation of mine—that is a very harsh attack on the Polish Church because she claims to impose in Poland's constitution a reference to Christian values and because in recent years she has claimed to impose by law Catholic morality in matters of abortion and so forth.

Look, I think that here there is an element of contradiction in a position that is anti-totalitarian but does not renounce an element of fundamentalism when it has the power to do so. In other words, it wants to impose by law, therefore on everyone, even those who are not believers, some moral convictions that are of believers only. And so, the self-criticism of Enlightenment thought is going very well, and everyone knows that this is one of the war-horses of much laicist thought, of the Frankfurt School, and so forth. However, repeating my promise that later I will send to Cardinal Ratzinger the many underlined passages in the encyclicals of this pope against Enlightenment thought, the criticism of Enlightenment thinking as a root of totalitarianism—that is precisely what this pope says—is identified by Wojtyła in the issue of relativism.

For the pope, and for the Church in general, along with Enlightenment thought relativism arises: relativism with respect to being and, above all, the relativism of values. And this relativism is seen as the cause of all evils. And, let us say, the incubator of forms of totalitarianism, and so we will have to discuss, then, this relativism, which, however, is also the basis of moral pluralism, without which there are no democratic societies. This pluralism is present here, too, and for this reason some maintain that it is in certain cases a very painful but legitimate choice. And, therefore, we will have to discuss this, too.

Lerner: Excuse me, because earlier I inadvertently caused confusion while introducing this question. Your choice, Your Eminence: Do you prefer to respond directly to him or ...

Ratzinger: Various questions, or rather, let us say, notes remain, both on the part of Professor Flores d'Arcais and from you, to which I have not responded. Therefore, it will be perhaps a bit difficult to respond briefly. I would nevertheless like to return to the problem of the rationality of the faith. It is true that Paul, on the one hand, acknowledges the evident character of the one God, but he is convinced, as am I, that one cannot rationally prove the divinity of Christ and therefore the Resurrection.

There is this, let us say, "excess" of the faith, but for someone who enters into it, a certain coherence is manifest, too, that is, the anticipation of rationality causes one to enter, and then, certainly, with this leap of faith it is nevertheless possible to see that these two spheres are not contradictory but form a unity with a logic of its own.

And as for Pascal, I would like to say for myself, as his reader, that it is not only this *plus* of the hope of immortality, but (as I understand this argument *du pari* [of the wager]) that he is then saying that experience (and here we see his century, also) is a condition for knowledge. If you make no attempt to gain knowledge of the Christian faith, it is logical that you cannot have knowledge. And so he says: Bet on reality, make the attempt, do the experiment, and then you will see the logic that is found in it. And this, too, seems to me something to examine more deeply, because here we are really on the terrain of the thought of the modern era.

Then I would like to say that, of course, I agree with the fact that it is in keeping with what I had said about the dictatorship of falsehood, in other words, that this sincerity of "yes is yes, no is no" is fundamental, it is man's vocation to truth, to sincerity; it is a fundamental saying of the Gospel. I listened with a bit of amazement when the professor told us that the rest was the work of the devil, and therefore he sees somewhat, it seems to me, the existence of the devil.

Lerner: But no doubt there are Christian roots even in Paolo Flores d'Arcais. The very fact that he describes the Gospel as a possible meeting ground—hah! I would never have been capable of saying that, obviously.

Ratzinger: Yes, I think perhaps that we will have to examine this argument again in greater depth, because the two points that he mentioned are important, but much more would have to be added.

Now, what you had said about the penitential liturgy, and the question that arises from this repentance concerning the concept of the Church herself, concerning her self-knowledge, is of great importance. And I think, as you do, that this liturgy of purification, of repentance, was a step that carries within it much more potential. And it is a duty of the Church and of theology to examine in depth this experience that is now also something on which to reflect.

We in the International Theological Commission gave it much thought, arriving at the diagnosis that it is still a little-explored territory that we must examine in depth. But we also understood, moreover, that even the Gospel always speaks to us about a Church of sinners and that this is precisely the uniqueness of this creature. And of Christ who came to call sinners with these words: tolerate even the weeds so as not to destroy the grain. And, therefore, the concept of Church willed by the Lord—today is the feast of Saint Matthew, to whom, since Matthew was a sinner, the Lord says explicitly: I came to call sinners—should be clarified much more, it seems to me. And, in any case, the purity of the Church comes not from her own merits; this is all too evident. If we look at Church history, it is an ongoing display of human weakness, and the paradox of the Church is that, despite all these failings, the Gospel lives and remains present.

And finally, now, I cannot discuss—because I am not well enough informed about it—what possible impositions of Christian values have been attempted by the Polish Church, but I would say two things: the first, if—and I say "if"; it is a hypothesis because I do not know the facts—perhaps some pressure was applied in Poland to include typically Christian values not necessarily shared by others, this is not to be attributed to the pope, I think.

Second point. It is of course—and now perhaps this will be an argument in our favor—not easy to distinguish correctly between typically Christian values, which are to be chosen only with the freedom of faith and cannot be imposed, and truly human values that concern the foundation of human dignity. And here the pope, and I too, we are convinced that abortion is not something that should be rejected only by Christians, because the sacredness of human life is in question, the right to exist comes before all the other rights. If I no longer have the right to live, what other right can I still have? And if it is true that these are human beings, the right is not a Christian imposition. But look, this is precisely the point: How can we verify that some values are simply human and not just Christian, even though in the past they were affirmed first by Christianity? (In ancient Greece, it was even normal to procure an abortion.) Perhaps by showing more clearly the evident character of the *human* value, which is not just a typically Christian one. Therefore—it seems to me—in these debates, which are also political, it would be important not to diagnose prematurely that Christians want to impose something. But, rather, really to discuss what is human and what is Christian.

Lerner: See, here there is no doubt that we are about to enter (and I am sure that Professor Flores d'Arcais is champing at the bit) into the alleged natural foundations of Christianity. And therefore: human values and faith values. But first I have a question, a clarification to ask from you and one that is extremely urgent for me, because of the interest that the topic of the penitential liturgy now holds for all of us. It was one of those moments of the Jubilee Year in which the Church spoke more directly also to outsiders, to others also, even to non-Catholics.

And therefore I would like to ask you this question: in several quarters—both among the most traditionalist who witnessed that penitential liturgy with uneasiness, and also among those who, conversely, were enthusiastic about it, in short, on both sides—people imagined somehow a subversive potential of this *mea culpa*. How can I put it: if the Church acknowledges the sins of her children against the Jews, against women, against native peoples, well then, it means that sooner or later, in a century or two, she will get around to acknowledging her sins with regard to homosexuals, separated couples, and sexual morality. [*To the audience:*] No, please: I think that this is a delicate topic that is not settled by applause.

Look, is there really a subversive potential in this purification of memory? Are there preconditions in it also for a hypothetical destabilization of some dogmas of faith?

Ratzinger: There is a critical potential, no doubt. But to talk about a subversive reality would not seem to me to be as suitable. Above all, I meant that with this liturgy the pope did not so much want to speak to the world, to offer a spectacle, as it were, of a penitent Church, but wanted to talk to God, and this seems to me very important: it was not designed as a demonstration to make an impression on the world. It made an impression precisely because that was not its intention and because it wanted, in the presence of God, and only in the light of God, to dare to say things that in themselves one dares to say only in the presence of God, but also *must* be said in the presence of God.

And I would say that the act was daring in this sense, that our conversation with God was visible to the world, but it was necessarily visible because the classic *Confiteor* of the Church, too, says: "*Confiteor*, I confess to God and to my brothers and sisters", because sin, which in the first place is a sin against God, is nevertheless always a sin against humanity, too.

And in God's light one can and must simply tell the whole truth, one must also say things that may appear dangerous and perhaps are, in the assurance that if they are said sincerely in God's presence and with a deep openness of conscience, God will use it for the good and will purify us. And so we can say that the effect, despite all the dangers involved, cannot be anything but positive.

Certainly I understand also the problems of the so-called traditionalists; bishops from the formerly Communist world told me: "We ourselves, too, are saying the things to which others had objected: they always undermined the Church, they always talked about all these evils, and by denigrating the Church in this way they tried to destroy confidence in the Church. And we defended our Church, which really was for them the refuge of the human person and of humanity, and therefore they did not believe those detractions. But some of the faithful believed, and now, after the fall of that dictatorship, if we say that they were right, what are we doing? The conscience of the little ones will suffer, and we are responsible for the little ones, too."

And it seems to me that these are reflections that we must respect, which have a weight of their own, and therefore the confession is justified only if it is performed in the presence of God, as a duty in God's presence, and in the sure confidence that God exists and responds.

Lerner: Thank you. Flores ...

Flores d'Arcais: The cardinal recalled specifically that the liturgy of repentance is something that concerns the Church first and foremost, rather than the world. And so I will limit myself to putting forward several reflections on this that I have read, put forward by believers who did see something important in this acknowledgment of serious sins of the past, fundamentally sins of intolerance—the Crusades, anti–Semitism, and so on—but who also saw limits and contradictions in this confession of the Church's past sins.

The first reflection is on the delay of these acknowledgments. Not so much on the fact that only today are the sins of hundreds or even thousands of years ago acknowledged, but on the fact that the Church decides so solemnly to acknowledge her own sins and then does not acknowledge what in the eyes of many Catholics appear to be present sins that are just as serious.

One thing was recalled by many Catholics: What sense does it make to recall many injustices that the Church defended in the past and not to recall—since the pope is the one who is speaking in the first person—something that that same pope committed? Namely, the famous appearance on the balcony in Santiago de Chile, beside General Pinochet, offering the Church's blessing to a criminal regime of butchers. [*Scattered applause.*]

No, excuse me, I would ask that ... These are questions ... We will not go that far on television, and therefore it is not that important ...

You see. And things of this sort could even be multiplied. Representatives of the Jewish communities maintained that the acknowledgment by the Church of her traditional anti–Semitism was too tepid and contradictory, and all the more contradictory when it is flatly contradicted by the elevation to the altars of a pope, Pius IX, who not only was a champion of the anti–laicism of the state, as everyone knows, of the most traditional integralism, the last pope-king—and I think that we will return to this topic—but also with the famous kidnapping of a Jewish boy blatantly sealed an attitude that certainly was not one of openness and tolerance with regard to the Roman Jews.

You see, then, once you decide so solemnly to do, not a self-criticism (those are political matters), but something much deeper for a Church, namely, the acknowledgment of her own sins, everything that is not acknowledged and yet is obvious is implicitly acknowledged as valid, as not sinful. Now, all this just casts a deep shadow on that celebration of repentance.

Lerner: Excuse me, "casts a deep shadow": But then why do you think that, during the two thousandth anniversary, this Church, this Theological Commission, and this pope decided to confess and to purify their memory with regard to that reality?

Flores d'Arcais: Because they want to acknowledge some of their sins that now, let us say, no longer cause scandal. To put it precisely—another topic that I think we will address later—as though they are calmly settling accounts today with Galileo but do not come to grips with contemporary molecular biology or Darwinism in its most recent developments.

And the question that you asked first, namely: Does this *mea culpa*, although partial and contradictory, by its logic not risk becoming subversive for the future? Look, here, too, I think that it should be said that an element of contradiction for the future will be fine with us, because this is the pope who—in *Veritatis Splendor*—dedicates almost an entire encyclical to a critique of theologies that are not perfectly aligned yet deeply widespread in the Catholic Church—not perfectly aligned with his Magisterium. Therefore, we say that it is a systematic and very precise *reprimand* of all the Catholic theological schools of thought that are considered to have gone too far.

At the same time, it is acknowledged that some things that in the past were affirmed by the Church as absolutely sacrosanct are now sins. And so the traditional Catholic or bishop is not entirely wrong when he says: "And tomorrow another pope will ask pardon for what today is affirmed instead as an absolute truth." I think that from this perspective we will have to discuss, maybe in the concluding part, what "a great pope" is understood to be, because naturally in many respects the present pope is a very great one. But other criteria—one of them: how many contradictions will he leave open in the bosom of the Church—perhaps will be topics to discuss later.

Lerner: Nobody said that leaving contradictions open is a sign of greatness.

I do not want to be so bold as to give you rules for your conduct, but to me it seems helpful, for the continuation of our discussion, not to go into particular actions of the pope concerning Pinochet, the beatification of Pius IX, in that we would run the risk ...

Of course, I allow complete freedom for Cardinal Ratzinger, if he also decides to go into questions about particular actions, but we are interested then in continuing the discussion in more general terms. Please.

Ratzinger: Yes, I agree, we cannot discuss all the details here, because precise information is lacking. Now that would not be a serious discussion, I think, to address all these individual points right now. I would not agree now, either, to evaluate the greatness of the pope. It is not our job now to judge the historical stature of the pope. Let us leave that to the future. I came for a philosophical discussion, and I read here topics that have not yet been discussed: faith and science, faith and theodicy, faith and Protestantism, other religions, divorce, abortion, and euthanasia (maybe we did touch on this), contraception and world hunger, faith and nihilism, etc. Therefore, now I would rather not leave the philosophical field and move to an area that is too historical, empirical, and contingent.

Lerner: Indeed, if you permit, I would like to take up again the preceding remarks by Cardinal Ratzinger, in which he alluded to the human principles, the natural laws to which the Church refers in affirming her own point of view, because here, perhaps, there may be a strong element of division. Here a nonbeliever, a non-Christian could—excuse the expression, but this is a question that I want to ask Paolo Flores—recognize an element of *arrogance*: How can you claim to assert that your viewpoint on abortion, bioethics, or family morality is not exclusively a religious viewpoint, a Christian viewpoint, but also refers directly to the natural laws? But I would say that since you have already expressed your view on this, let us hear first Professor Flores, since this point seems to me decisive in your regard.

Flores d'Arcais: This is a crucial question. Then, of course, there is also the problem of science and faith: we will have to address it by going backward, toward the foundations. But I think that this is the key to all the possible differences of opinion. Namely: Christianity maintains that its truths are at the same time the natural truths. Not all its truths: there are then other truths to which reason cannot arrive. But certainly "right reason" cannot enter into conflict, cannot say things different from what the Catholic faith says. In a case where reason arrived at contrary conclusions, it would try to say that it is not "right reason" but, rather, reason that is incoherent, in other words, not functioning. And this gives rise to all sorts of conflicts.

The key to all this is the idea of natural law, natural moral law. The natural and moral norm is said to be inscribed already in being, in reality itself. Natural norms are said to constitute a sort of chromosomes of the universe and of reality. For this reason, it is said to be merely a matter of discovering them with our reason and obeying these norms.

I think that this is absolutely false and untenable. I think that there is no natural law, that there are many human laws, which often over the course of history have common traits but which never all have common traits, and that therefore the claim to identify a particular morality with a natural law, however lofty and noble it may be, brings with it all the risks of intolerance. Why do I think that we cannot talk about a natural law? We understand "natural" to refer to human nature. If by natural law we understand something that all human beings in fact have known was bad, even if they then violated it: hah, that something does not exist. In his history, man has considered entirely different things to be valid or even supreme norms—and over the course of human history, these moral norms were almost always religious norms as well. Not even the prohibition of homicide was considered a natural norm.

Here I would like again to cite a quotation from Pascal that I always use, because Pascal is precisely the one who says: Man has considered every norm and its opposite to be worthy of veneration. And he makes a list (patricide, incest, etc.) of terrible things, saying: there are men who have considered them values; not only did they tolerate them, but they actually considered them values.

On the other hand, in many primitive societies—they, too, were human beings—ritual cannibalism was considered an ethical and religious duty. And we could continue. Therefore, if by nature we mean what is normally meant, that is, everyone belonging to the species *homo sapiens*, certainly there is not one norm that was always shared by all human beings. I repeat: not in the sense that they knew what was good but they violated the law, but, rather, in the sense that they did not consider it good; they considered things that were quite different and incompatible with one another to be good.

Then in what sense do we say "natural law"? If we establish *a priori* that one part of humanity was against nature and the other part—coincidentally the one that shares our norms—was true humanity, we perform an operation that each one of us can perform, with his values, but which has as it consequence saying that someone who did not or does not share those values not only sins but is actually outside of humanity. This is the logical consequence of it.

I imagine that we will then look more closely at the individual headings of this disagreement. Let us take—just to mention it, then we will look more closely at it—the element of the natural law that is most debated in recent years: the question of abortion. This was referred to earlier. For a Christian, abortion is a crime, and the Christian says: I say this not only by faith; I think that I can prove it rationally.

As a matter of principle, this is true; at any rate, there are also some nonbelievers against the possibility of abortion. (I recall that in his day Norberto Bobbio [an Italian political scientist and journalist] was one of them, though not very rigidly.) And nevertheless there are many, many others who are convinced that they can prove that, arguing rationally, abortion is a very difficult thing but is not a homicide and has nothing to do with infanticide. So true is this that for centuries even in the Catholic Church it was debated. There are texts in which Saint Augustine, who maintained that from the first moment there was already a soul in the mother's womb, argued harshly with many bishops of his era. And from Augustine's words we understand that those bishops must have been in the majority, that they maintained that, instead, the soul entered only in the third month of gestation and that therefore until the third month there was no human being; and therefore there was no crime, either, in aborting.

This is to say that the question was debated for a long time even in the Church.

Now, the persons present here who maintain that, although painful and certainly not [to be used] as a mere means of contraception, abortion is, however, not a crime; are they therefore irrational, anti-human?

In this way, we determine that anyone who argues— often, I think, with the best, most convincing reasons— against the Church's viewpoint is without rationality and without humanity. For this reason, the crime starts from the first day of gestation, even though the embryo, as you know (but we will return to this also) in the first sixteen days is still made up of undifferentiated cells.

Look, I think that this idea of natural law can be the source of an abusive claim, because it considers *a priori* irrational and inhumane anyone who argues—and acts according to reason that is *not right*—in a contrary way. And simply claims to make "universal" and "human" coincide with something that is, instead, one of many moral viewpoints that have appeared in history. Back to you.

Ratzinger: This is a point on which there is already a printed debate between Flores d'Arcais and me, in which

Flores d'Arcais harshly condemned a passage from the encyclical—I'm not sure now—*Evangelium Vitae*, and perhaps also *Fides et Ratio*, in which the Holy Father says: There are some things about which a majority cannot decide, because at stake are values that are not subject to shifting majorities; there are some things where the majority's right to decide ends, because it is a matter of humanity, respect for the human being as such.

And Flores d'Arcais responded: Here the pope proves to be really anti-Enlightenment—now I remember: it was in the encyclical *Fides et Ratio*—and proves that with this philosophy he has nothing to say to philosophy, to today's culture, because it is opposed to this contemporary culture.

To this I responded that I decisively defend the fact that there are values not subject to the opinion and free will of majorities. We Germans have a very powerful example, as was said, because we decided that there is such a thing as life that is not worth living and, therefore, we have the right to cleanse the world of these unworthy lives so as to create the pure race and the superior man of the future.

Here the Nuremberg Court after the war correctly said that there are rights that are not debatable for any government. Even if an entire nation were to make the decision, nevertheless, it remains unjust to do that. And therefore, they could justly condemn persons who had carried out the laws of a state that had been issued formally and correctly. That is to say, there are values—and I think that precisely this is also a result of Enlightenment thinking: the declaration (finally in 1948 with greater precision) of inviolable human rights that are valid for everyone in all circumstances. It was a great advance of humanity, and we must not lose it.

Therefore, I do not agree with that historical argument, in other words, that in history for every value there is also a contrary position, and there is nothing considered a crime by one civilization that was not considered in another as a value to be put into practice. This statistical fact [only] proves the problem of human history and proves the fallibility of the human being.

Along these lines, Origen, a Father of the Church, had said in the early third century: I know that in the Black Sea writings there are laws that legitimize crimes, and, if someone lives in that context, he must rebel against the law, because there is an absolutely inviolable reality to which laws cannot be opposed, and the laws that do oppose it are bad ones.

And this seems clear to me: at least we know now, after this century and its horrors, that there is such a thing as the absolute sacredness of human life and that laws that always existed in the world that oppose this inviolability of man's dignity and of the rights that follow from this dignity are unjust, even if they are decided and issued in a formally correct manner.

Therefore it seems to me that this claim (that the majority has no say in certain matters but must respect what is human) is fundamental for the future of our civilization.

Another question. Two more questions.

The first is: What is the foundation of this inviolability of some rights? Catholic tradition says: it is creation. They then introduced, from Greek philosophy, the word "nature": *physis*. And maybe this word could be replaced with a better word, I would rather not discuss terminology here. Nevertheless, the idea was that *physis*, nature, is not the product of blind chance, of blind evolution, but that, notwithstanding the course of evolution, there is a reason behind it, and therefore there is a morality of being itself.

I thought that that expression of Flores d'Arcais was very beautiful: that the moral elements were present, so to speak, in the chromosomes of reality. This does not mean that empirical nature must be canonized as the natural law but that there is a priority of the spirit over irrationality, and, therefore, there is a moral foundation that bars some actions.

Therefore this is the first point: What is the foundation of the inviolability of some rights and of the inadmissibility of some laws, what is the foundation of this limit of our legislative power? We say creation, the fact of coming from a mind, from a *logos*.

Whether Flores d'Arcais has another answer, well, we will see. The second question is how to identify those things that are inviolable and have precedence over our legislation and therefore protect the dignity of man. And this of course is difficult, and here errors can creep in, hasty identifications.

Now I would not like to enter into a debate—we are all familiar with it—about abortion, but only to say: although Saint Augustine, with a kind of natural science of his time, was convinced, as was Saint Thomas later with Aristotle, that animation occurs only after a certain lapse of time and, before that, the thing without a soul is not an individual human being, this does not call into question the principle that no human being—just because he is weak and just because he is defenseless and does not yet have the use of reason—can be killed. The empirical problem is when the human being begins.

For Augustine, and I hope for all of us, it is absolutely certain: if someone is a human being, he is inviolable. Then the other question is: When is someone a human being? We all know today that this Aristotelian science that sees animation after three or six months is not correct. And, according to my biological inquiries, in reality from the first moment this being carries within itself a complete program of a human being that then develops. But the program is such that we can therefore speak about an individual. And we cannot dogmatize a result of the natural sciences, and therefore we have said that of course we await further findings, we do not want to dogmatize what currently appears to be the most convincing, best documented position.

But, we have said, therefore, even if these positions were not right, there is at least a valid hypothesis, a well-founded probability or at least possibility that there could already be a human being. And already this probability—if not certainty, but probability—no longer permits us to kill this being, because probably at least, or possibly, it is a human being. This is our logic on this point.

Lerner: Be patient, Your Eminence, but this is really a question that I want to ask you. The Church and Christianity have not always attributed such a central value to the defense of human life. You cited Saint Augustine before; in Saint Augustine's era, in past eras, the defense of human life was not as crucial, as central as it has become today in the affairs of the Church. Or am I wrong?

Ratzinger: The Church then must learn, and, precisely with regard to human rights, we have learned also from Enlightenment thought another ...

Lerner: I was not referring only to Enlightenment thought. I would like to quote for you, if you allow me, the objection of a laicist Italian thinker, Gian Enrico Rusconi, who, although he identifies himself as a Catholic, was a believer who reflects today on the crisis—which he describes as parallel—of laicist thought and of Catholic theology. Rusconi maintains that there is a serious crisis in that this insistent reference of theology to the natural laws is in fact a way of clinging to a diminishment of principles, of certainties, of the solidity of the past. And also this centrality of the defense of human life in doctrine is in fact a recent acquisition and not something absolute from the past, from Church history.

Ratzinger: I would say two things. The first point: there was a certain excess in the use of the natural law in the Church's social doctrine that arose in the late nineteenth century. And then in the twentieth century, until Vatican Council II, there were excesses. But this fact that there was a little, let us say, exuberance does not change the fact that it is still there in the writings of Saint Paul, who speaks about *katanoesis* [discernment, perception].

There was respect for creation and the deep conviction that creation speaks about God and, therefore, speaks about man. We find it also in the Old Testament; therefore, I would say that we can very well and must debate about the expansion of the natural law—how far does it extend?—but as for the fact that Christians have always considered creation to be a reality in which the *logos* is present—and therefore not only a mathematical structure but also an indication of the righteous life—this really is a heritage from the very beginning.

It is true also that concern about the defense of human life is greater today than in the past and, in this sense, is also a specific feature of our century, in which, however, we experienced a cruelty and a contempt for the human being that ought to be a wake-up call for us. But I would say that the Christianity never thought that man could dispose of a human being, of human life.

A different matter is the problem of the death penalty, which could be thought of as a concession to protect society and also to expiate a sin. But even if these thoughts existed, the idea that in certain circumstances—by means of a proportionalism of values—one could dispose of human life, that was never the case.

Flores d'Arcais: I share absolutely the view that a majority is not enough to decide any matter whatsoever.

Moreover, I think that we must be clear about the fact that precisely in democracy, where majority rule is the fundamental instrument for making decisions—even and especially in democracy—it is not true that the majority can make any decision whatsoever. It is no accident that modern democracies are founded on constitutions that set limits for any majority to decide what it wants. In general, all modern constitutions accept those human or civil rights that arose from the great revolutions (English, American, and French), which indeed declared certain rights of each individual to be inalienable.

Therefore, from this perspective, our agreement is total. The problem is, about what things can majorities not decide? In other words: What foundation do these human or civil rights have, and who establishes it?

Lerner: For example, pardon the interruption, if a majority tried to reinstate the death penalty in Italy, do you think that that would be licit?

Flores d'Arcais: Our constitution says no. Of course it would be necessary first to change the constitution, the mechanisms for changing the constitution and then ... As things stand now, the fundamental norm of our coexistence ...

Lerner: So in the final analysis: yes, if the constitution were modified ...

Flores d'Arcais: No, just a minute …

Lerner: Would it be conceivable?

Flores d'Arcais: Let's not make it just a question about constitutional procedures, because then we could reach that point, but the questions that Cardinal Ratzinger asked go far beyond constitutional procedures.

So, we agree that a majority cannot always and in any way decide about everything. The problem is: About what matters can it not decide, that is, what is the core of truly inalienable shared values that cannot be touched? First point. Second point: What are these inalienable rights of each individual based on? Point three: Who establishes them?

Now, Cardinal Ratzinger said in an absolutely explicit way that the foundation of those rights that are called natural rights is not nature, a term that could be equivocal, but he said explicitly: it is creation. This is the foundation of a core of rights and duties that no majority can touch. And this is absolutely problematic, because establishing that creation is the untouchable core of values, and therefore of the rights and duties of each one of us, means establishing a religious prejudice. Which, in a society that is no longer founded on religion as its first principle, does not hold.

Creation is certain for those who believe—not for all the religions in existence today, but, let us say, certainly for the three major religions of the Book. But it is simply imaginary, let us call it that, for those who do not believe.

Lerner: Here, too, I must take the liberty of another interruption, though. Based on the coherence of the shared values of our society, there is an almost unanimous judgment to acknowledge (and it is no accident that we often speak about a Judeo-Christian society, even understood in a nonreligious sense) the Ten Commandments, which are certainly not the natural law; they are revelations. So. Does Paolo Flores accept them as elements of coherence, as a common mortar—not of this auditorium, of this table—but of our life together?

Flores d'Arcais: We will get to that, too, because the questions are multiplying.

But therefore the fundamental thing is: if the foundation of these natural rights and duties, among which is the inviolability of human life, truly were creation, I think that it would be an extremely fragile foundation, because it would concern only those who believe in creation.

Now, the majority of people who live in Western societies do not in fact believe in creation, they believe that everything came to be according to a certain cosmological development ...

Lerner: Let us say that most times the question is not asked, because that is the truth.

Flores d'Arcais: That is not true. I think that we live in a superficial era, but not that superficial. I do not think that this question is not asked. I think that in some way, and often, it is asked.

However, we are asking it. Certainly the idea of creation cannot be the foundation of a pluralistic society in which many do not believe and many think that the universe in which we live resulted from the famous Big Bang and had a development that was not determined *a priori*. Science, through its most recent advances, tells us that there was an evolution of the universe that was not established *a priori* and could have taken other paths.

One of the great science writers, Stephen Jay Gould, has reconstructed precisely seven crucial moments of evolution, from the Big Bang to the birth of man, in which evolution could have taken totally different directions, and, he says, if it had taken them—and there was no probability in favor of the one that it took, it could have taken others—we would not be here to discuss it.

Therefore, from this perspective, scientists today acknowledge what a very great biologist of our time, Jacques Monod, said a few decades ago, that is: we are the product of chance and of necessity.

And so, we cannot place creation at the foundation of these inalienable rights and duties. This is why I think that today we cannot say: they are human rights. We must have the courage to acknowledge that they are civil rights, which does not make them any less indispensable, but makes us understand that in order to assert themselves—two or three centuries ago—these values needed a sort of laicist religion, in other words, [they needed] to say that they are connatural with human nature.

In reality, they were so little connatural with human nature that man lived for millennia trampling on them, and it took very difficult struggles, sacrifices of generations upon generations, to have them acknowledged provisionally. And they are so uncertain that every day we read in the newspapers, even here at home [in Italy], about violations of those civil rights.

They are civil rights, that is, they are a choice that we have made on which to found our life together. And they are, in a certain respect—of course, also in a decisive respect—the result of the secularization of some Christian values. But they do not lead to such obvious and incontestable consequences. The example of abortion has been cited, and maybe there will be other even more tragic ones. In this regard: not only would many persons certainly have trouble going to dinner with someone who calmly boasted and related that he had done away with various persons, slaughtered children, I don't know ... I think that none of us would agree to go to dinner, for example, with an ex-SS officer who told us about how he used to throw Jewish children into the crematoriums. But I also maintain that, in contrast, normally, we go to dinner with persons who have had abortions, but, whether we agree or not (we know that in some cases these were painful decisions), we do not think at all that we are going to dinner with murderers.

And so, first of all it is certain that there is a deep, widespread rational conviction that murder and abortion are not on the same level. Certainly, for someone who believes in creation—not only in creation, but in a whole series, then, of interpretations of creation—this can be true, because there would be not only this disagreement between those who believe and those who do not believe about what homicide is. Moreover, the idea of considering an abortion homicide is repugnant to me: never, never would I consider it by the same standard. And I, personally, also regard as immoral anyone who maintains something of that sort.

So, it is not even enough to be Christian—and therefore not only to believe in creation, but to believe in creation by a God who then was incarnate in his Son Jesus Christ, who died on the Cross and rose again and so forth—it is not even enough to believe all that, in order to arrive at the same conclusion on the question of life.

You see how absurd it is to claim that a viewpoint of one form of Christianity coincides with the natural norm. It is a claim that inevitably leads to a refusal to recognize pluralism.

Lerner: I fear, Paolo, that we will not manage to address further all the topics that you have raised, because it is already getting late, but I think that it is fair to give ...

Ratzinger: Yes, I am grateful for this observation, and I would like to be brief, because in reality, since I have reached the third age in life, I feel a bit tired.

But to respond briefly: I sought to show the reason why, for a Christian, the idea of the priority of reason over matter, therefore of the presence of reason in matter, and therefore creation would be something about which one could speak, beyond the limits of the faith. But of course Flores d'Arcais is right, this conviction about creation is not shared by everyone.

In this sense, it would not be a foundation that could lead to a common action, because this was the case already in antiquity, that is, the Fathers of the Church translated a word of faith into a philosophical word, "nature", which is not a word of faith but a word of philosophy, and they agreed on this point with Stoicism, which did not know of a creator, or of a creation, but saw a certain, let us say, divine quality in being itself and a message that was valid for everyone. And for this reason, then, the word "nature" was an applicable vehicle that was accessible beyond the limits of the faith. And this is the reason why the word "nature" entered into the vocabulary of theology, of the Magisterium, as an indication of the philosophical element that in itself is also separable from a deeper vision of the faith. In this sense, it seems to me, in the future, too, it will be necessary to discuss the usefulness and reasonableness of this concept "nature", which expresses the conviction that realities carry within themselves a moral message and set limits on our arrangements.

And it seems to me that the ecological movement, faced with all the destruction in the world and the dangers that threaten us, has understood this: that nature brings us a message, and we must be attentive to this message of nature. And I think that perhaps, today, precisely with our experiences of a nature that has been abused, we can, in a new way, understand this common concept that is a concept of reason and of experience, be more attentive to this message that gives us a foundation for our action and shows also a limit to our free will.

And therefore I cannot agree that these inviolable rights stated by those major documents, the product of the Enlightenment, are only civil rights, our own choices. If they are our choices they can be changed. And they must not be changed so as not to destroy humanity and the sense of respect for the other. And the argument that centuries, maybe thousands of years, did not live out these values, and therefore they could not be natural, does not count for me, because man is capable of living against nature, and we see it.

But the fact that man does not want to accept nature's message does not imply that it is not really a message. It seems to me that it should not be so difficult to understand that man is a creature, a special being that bears within himself a dignity that we must always respect in the other, even if he appears to us to be without great value, disagreeable, or something different.

And I would like to say another thing. Flores d'Arcais said that someone who considers abortion to be homicide commits an immoral act. I do not accept this. I can understand his hesitations on this point, but that it is in itself obvious that this is a very weak, dependent human being and therefore to kill it is to kill a man—it seems to me that to say this cannot be characterized as immoral and thus make an appeal to the conscience, to the reflection of the other party.

And therefore, finally, they say that none of the Christian values is a value that should be held as a common value, whether or not we call them Christian; these human rights, which are, I think, the proper foundation of Enlightenment civilization, matured in Christianity but are really human values and are the great heritage of our civilization, which we should defend with all our heart and with all our reason.

Lerner: Look, these two hours have truly flown by, and I realize that we would like to continue yet for a long time. No, don't get up, because if Cardinal Ratzinger allows me, I feel the need to ask each of you a concluding question, no more than that. Paolo Flores d'Arcais says that he has had one less chance to speak, but we want to point out, too, that it is such a rare occasion to have Cardinal Ratzinger here that I will take advantage of it.

Flores d'Arcais: Okay ...

Lerner: The question for Paolo Flores, in conclusion, is precisely the one that is probably at the origin of his choice to dedicate an issue [with a print run] of a hundred thousand copies of his magazine to this discussion and to this debate.

Behind it, Paolo, isn't there the sense of experiencing a moment of weakness of Enlightenment and laicist thought, which in two centuries has not succeeded in extinguishing religious faith or relegating it to a residual position (indeed, it has contributed to its development), but today finds itself again faced with it as a strong system of thought? How is it that you feel the need to confront this strong system of thought and also to dispute it at every step of the way?

Flores d'Arcais: But I said this at the beginning. I have no ambition, and I think that no laicist or atheist thinker has one, to make religious conviction something residual.

This truly was a part, I won't say of Enlightenment thought—because the Enlightenment thinkers were almost all believers, not in a particular religion, but certainly in a creator God, and so forth—but I would consider ridiculous and bizarre the idea of a commitment to "convert away from the faith" those who believe. There are much more exciting things in life than that to which to dedicate oneself.

The need to discuss with those who believe, in my opinion, springs precisely from the many topics that, I regret, we cannot continue to dissect, which can lead to irremediable conflicts and to risks of intolerance, just when faith claims to be not only faith but also the fulfillment of reason.

I concluded this essay in *MicroMega* by acknowledging outright that today, with respect to one fundamental question—support of the marginalized, the least ones, the duty of solidarity—believers give nonbelievers many points to ponder. And probably not having a faith makes it much more difficult to renounce egotism, to sacrifice oneself for others. I do not mean that it makes it impossible. A laicist friend told me: But why ignore the fact that it can be done? There are many nonbelievers who have sacrificed their lives for some values. And it is quite true.

We live in a democracy thanks to many nonbelievers who fifty years ago sacrificed their lives, at a young age, too—thinking that it was the only life and that with it everything would end—and sacrificed it in order to give us a democratic future against fascism. Therefore, consider whether a laicist or an atheist can sacrifice his own life.

But I have the impression that it is easier, that is, less difficult to sacrifice it in exceptional moments than it is to make little sacrifices but daily ones—for those who do not believe than for those who believe, or at least for some who do not believe. It is a fact that today the majority of volunteers, which I think is one of the few truly positive phenomena in our society, the large majority is made up of believers, even though obviously there are also nonbelievers, not only in Italy but also in the world. Think, for example, of the institution Doctors Without Borders.

That being said, however, I am still of the opinion that it is fundamentally important to arrive at a basic clarification of one claim that, in all the basic questions touched on by Cardinal Ratzinger, returned to make a fleeting appearance: as long as those who have faith think that this faith is also one with reason, in other words, that by arguing rationally one cannot arrive at truths or opinions in conflict with it, the temptation to impose itself, when it can—and to impose itself with force, also—will always exist.

Because, you see, it makes no sense to say that nature gives us a message. Nature, alas, does not give us any message. Fortunately, some minorities, in the most recent era, especially as far as ecology is concerned, in the past generation, have begun to pose for themselves the problem of the fact that nature, which still tells us nothing, is not inexhaustible. But this is not something that nature said, because nature says absolutely nothing; it is something on which we have reflected, fortunately.

And so, this idea of thinking that there are things that we should avoid changing, only if we think that they are the dictates of nature and not a conscious choice of ours, I think that it is utterly irresponsible and undermines responsibility. In order to defend this core of indispensable values, we must not think that they are inscribed in nature, because this leads us to think that—since they are inscribed in nature—sooner or later they will be acknowledged.

No. They are not inscribed in nature at all; they are the result of an extremely laborious historical evolution and of sacrifices by generations of persons. And precisely for this reason, because we want them to be indispensable and can defend them uncompromisingly, day by day. Because we know that we are totally responsible for these values.

To think that they are already inscribed in the cosmos is to undermine our responsibility and is to make room, I think, for recurrences that we absolutely want to avoid. That being said, I am very sorry that we must conclude here, I would have liked to be able to discuss with Cardinal Ratzinger many other questions connected with the matters that we are discussing, but I am sure that there will be other occasions. Certainly *MicroMega* continues to be at the disposal of his viewpoint, too, which still does not convince me.

Lerner: Well, now, very correctly, by way of symmetry, Cardinal Ratzinger told me earlier: Let us leave the last word to Professor Flores. But if you allow me ... If I may make so bold, and I do this because first in private I asked permission to do so, I would just like to ask you a final question that perhaps departs a bit from this debate that we have experienced this evening.

In the same text of the speech at the Sorbonne that was republished also in *MicroMega*, referring to the profound crisis—these are the words that it uses—of European Christianity and advocating, in reference to this very crisis, the need to restore the element of truth of the *religio vera* as the key element, he makes references to Vatican

Council II, defined as an event that caused an enormous upheaval in the Catholic Church. These are his words: A surgical operation that is not necessarily equivalent to a cure. Here I make so bold as to ask a question that has a personal character, also, because it is well known that the young Bishop Ratzinger ...

Ratzinger: Not a bishop ...

Lerner: Not yet a bishop, the young theologian Ratzinger participated enthusiastically in the work of that council and was also an element thereof that was—let us say— strongly in favor of innovation. Does Cardinal Ratzinger, forty years later, see in that event one of the elements of the crisis of European Christianity? In other words, has there been a change in you?

Ratzinger: A change, no. I still think that this engagement was necessary, that it was the moment to open up new paths of theological language and thought, and to seek a new encounter with the world and a new depth of the faith, especially, too, in the dialogue with our brethren, the non-Catholic Churches.

In this sense, it seem to me that it was a providential, necessary event, but with this comparison to a surgical operation I wanted to show also that a beneficial event does not necessarily immediately imply the positive effects that are hoped for. And I have a great predecessor, the theologian Gregory Nazianzen, who is called precisely the Theologian; when invited by the emperor to the Council of Constantinople, after the previous experiences that he had had with other councils, he said: I will never again go to a council, because it only creates confusion. Such was his desperation.

I would not say that; *he* was the one who said it. A council, as a message, as an action, let us say as a profound intervention in the life of the Church, is necessary, but at the same time it also causes new complications ... and we are in a phase in which we must confront these complications.

Flores d'Arcais: Also because in those councils, the emperors ended up deciding; fortunately, today the bishops decide instead.

Lerner: Sincere thanks to all for this very beautiful evening.

INDEX